5-ingredient SLOW COOKER recipes

Better Homes and Gardens® Books
Des Moines, Iowa

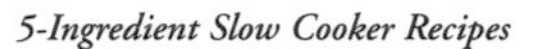
5-Ingredient Slow Cooker Recipes
Editor: Carrie E. Holcomb
Contributing Editors: Joyce R. Trollope, Mary Williams
Contributing Writer: Cynthia Pearson
Senior Associate Design Director: Mick Schnepf
Contributing Designer: Brad Ruppert, Studio G
Copy Chief: Terri Fredrickson
Publishing Operations Manager: Karen Schirm
Book Production Managers: Pam Kvitne, Marjorie J. Schenkelberg, Rick von Holdt, Mark Weaver
Contributing Copy Editor: Kim Catanzarite
Contributing Proofreaders: Alison Crouch, Maria Duryée, Gretchen Kauffman
Indexer: Kathleen Poole
Editorial Assistants: Cheryl Eckert, Karen McFadden
Edit and Design Production Coordinator: Mary Lee Gavin
Test Kitchen Director: Lynn Blanchard
Test Kitchen Product Supervisor: Lori Wilson
Test Kitchen Home Economists: Paige Boyle; Marilyn Cornelius; Juliana Hale; Laura Harms, R.D.; Jennifer Kalinowski, R.D.; Maryellyn Krantz; Jill Moberly; Dianna Nolin; Colleen Weeden; Charles Worthington
Recipe Developers: Tami Leonard, Shelli McConnell, Marcia Stanley

Meredith® Books
Editor in Chief: Linda Raglan Cunningham
Design Director: Matt Strelecki
Managing Editor: Gregory H. Kayko
Executive Editor: Jennifer Dorland Darling

Publisher: James D. Blume
Executive Director, Marketing: Jeffrey Myers
Executive Director, New Business Development: Todd M. Davis
Executive Director, Sales: Ken Zagor
Director, Operations: George A. Susral
Director, Production: Douglas M. Johnston
Business Director: Jim Leonard

Vice President and General Manager: Douglas J. Guendel

***Better Homes and Gardens®* Magazine**
Editor in Chief: Karol DeWulf Nickell
Deputy Editor, Food and Entertaining: Nancy Hopkins

Meredith Publishing Group
President, Publishing Group: Stephen M. Lacy
Vice President-Publishing Director: Bob Mate

Meredith Corporation
Chairman and Chief Executive Officer: William T. Kerr

In Memoriam: E.T. Meredith III (1933-2003)

Our seal assures you that every recipe in *5-Ingredient Slow Cooker Recipes* has been tested in the Better Homes and Gardens® Test Kitchen. This means that each recipe is practical and reliable, and meets our high standards of taste appeal. We guarantee your satisfaction with this book for as long as you own it.

Library of Congress Control Number: 2004102148
ISBN: 0-696-22089-X

All of us at Meredith® Books are dedicated to providing you with the information and ideas you need to create delicious foods. We welcome your comments and suggestions. Write to us at: Meredith Books, Cookbook Editorial Department, 1716 Locust St., Des Moines, IA 50309-3023.

If you would like to purchase any of our cooking, crafts, gardening, home improvement, or home decorating and design books, check wherever quality books are sold. Or visit us at: bhgbooks.com

Table of Contents

Introduction

Your day is busy and hours designated to the kitchen limited. But that's not so for your slow cooker. Use this *5-Ingredient Slow Cooker Recipes* cookbook and your family is served home-cooked food that's big on taste—with minimal effort!

Shopping is easy with short lists of smart ingredients. Prep is accomplished in minutes. Whether you arrive home hungry after a full day at work or play, or need to turn out a huge meal from a small kitchen, five-ingredient slow-cook recipes are your secret solution to tantalizing food that's ready and waiting.

How to count the ingredients in these recipes:

The following are not counted:
- Water
- Nonstick cooking spray
- Ingredients listed as optional

Salt and pepper are counted as one ingredient.

Types of Slow Cooking Appliances:

A continuous slow cooker/crockery cooker cooks foods at a very low wattage. Heating coils or elements wrap around the sides of the cooker and remain on continuously. This appliance has two fixed settings—low and high—and some models automatically shift from high to low. The ceramic liner may or may not be removable. All the slow cooker recipes in this book were tested in this type of appliance. With each recipe, we recommend the slow cooker sizes that will work best.

An intermittent slow cooker has the heating element located below the food container. It cycles on and off during operation and has a dial indicating temperatures in degrees. Because recipes in this book need continuous slow cooking, they will not cook properly in this type of appliance.

1

Steaming Soups and Stews

Beefy Borscht

Borscht, the long popular sweet-sour soup hailing from Eastern Europe, has a rich and varied history. A scoop of sour cream takes it to the next level of delight.

Prep: 15 minutes Cook: Low 8 hours, High 4 hours Makes: 6 main-dish servings (8 cups)

12 ounces boneless beef chuck, cut into ½-inch cubes
4 cups water
1 16-ounce jar red cabbage, undrained
1 15- to 16-ounce can diced beets, drained
1 envelope (½ of a 2-ounce package) onion soup mix
½ cup dairy sour cream

1 Place meat in a 3½- or 4-quart slow cooker. Add water, undrained cabbage, drained beets, and onion soup mix to cooker.

2 Cover and cook on low-heat setting for 8 to 10 hours or on high-heat setting for 4 to 5 hours. Ladle soup into bowls. Top with sour cream.

Nutrition Facts per serving: 171 cal., 6 g total fat (3 g sat. fat), 41 mg chol., 794 mg sodium, 14 g carbo., 1 g fiber, 13 g pro.
Daily Values: 3% vit. A, 9% vit. C, 3% calcium, 10% iron

Beef and Barley Soup

Not familiar with pearl barley? Look for it next to the rice at your local supermarket.

Prep: 15 minutes Cook: Low 7 hours, High 3½ hours Makes: 4 main-dish servings (6 cups)

Nonstick cooking spray
12 ounces boneless beef chuck, cut into ½-inch cubes
4 cups water
1 10½-ounce can condensed French onion soup
1 cup purchased shredded carrot
½ cup medium pearl barley
1 teaspoon dried thyme or oregano, crushed

1 Coat a large skillet with cooking spray. Heat over medium heat. In hot skillet cook meat until brown. Drain off fat.

2 In a 3½- to 4½-quart slow cooker combine the meat, water, soup, carrot, barley, and thyme.

3 Cover and cook on low-heat setting for 7 to 8 hours or on high-heat setting for 3½ to 4 hours. Season to taste with salt and black pepper.

Nutrition Facts per serving: 252 cal., 5 g total fat (1 g sat. fat), 52 mg chol., 684 mg sodium, 29 g carbo., 5 g fiber, 22 g pro.
Daily Values: 156% vit. A, 7% vit. C, 4% calcium, 18% iron

Minestrone Plus

Ordinary canned soup becomes extraordinary when slow cooked with your choice of beef, pork, or sausage. Come the end of the day, all you have to do is add some cheese.

Prep: 20 minutes Cook: Low 7 hours, High 3½ hours Makes: 6 main-dish servings (10 cups)

- 1 pound lean ground beef, ground pork, or sweet Italian sausage
- ½ cup chopped onion (1 medium)
- 2 19-ounce cans ready-to-serve chunky minestrone soup
- 1 15½-ounce can navy beans, rinsed and drained
- 2 cups water
- ¼ cup finely shredded Parmesan cheese (1 ounce)

1 In a large skillet cook ground meat and onion until meat is brown. Drain off fat.

2 In a 3½- or 4-quart slow cooker combine cooked meat mixture, minestrone, navy beans, and water.

3 Cover and cook on low-heat setting for 7 to 8 hours or on high-heat setting for 3½ to 4 hours. Ladle soup into bowls. Sprinkle with Parmesan cheese.

Nutrition Facts per serving: 424 cal., 18 g total fat (9 g sat. fat), 67 mg chol., 1,408 mg sodium, 33 g carbo., 8 g fiber, 33 g pro.
Daily Values: 68% vit. A, 8% vit. C, 37% calcium, 24% iron

Taco Soup

If you like, top this soup with crunchy tortilla chips and creamy shredded cheese. It's a refreshing twist on the traditional presentation.

Prep: 15 minutes Cook: Low 6 hours, High 3 hours
Makes: 4 to 6 main-dish servings (about 8 cups)

- 1 pound lean ground beef
- 3 cups water
- 1 15- to 16-ounce can red kidney beans, rinsed and drained
- 1 14½-ounce can Mexican-style stewed tomatoes, undrained
- 1 10¾-ounce can condensed tomato soup
- 1 1.25-ounce package taco seasoning mix
- Crushed tortilla chips (optional)
- Shredded Monterey Jack cheese (optional)

1 In a large skillet cook ground meat until brown. Drain off fat.

2 In a 3½- or 4-quart slow cooker combine meat, water, beans, undrained tomatoes, tomato soup, and taco seasoning mix.

3 Cover and cook on low-heat setting for 6 to 8 hours or on high-heat setting for 3 to 4 hours. Ladle soup into bowls. If desired, sprinkle with tortilla chips and shredded cheese.

Nutrition Facts per serving: 456 cal., 23 g total fat (8 g sat. fat), 78 mg chol., 2,092 mg sodium, 36 g carbo., 6 g fiber, 31 g pro.
Daily Values: 8% vit. A, 82% vit. C, 6% calcium, 27% iron

Beef and Bean Ragout

A ragout is a rich, well-seasoned stew. Beans and beef star in this tasty version.

Prep: 10 minutes Cook: Low 8 hours, High 4 hours Makes: 6 main-dish servings (7 cups)

1 pound beef stew meat, cut into 1-inch cubes
1 16-ounce can kidney beans, rinsed and drained
1 15-ounce can tomato sauce with onion and garlic
1 14½-ounce can Italian-style stewed tomatoes, undrained
½ of a 28-ounce package frozen loose-pack diced hash brown potatoes with onion and peppers (about 4 cups)

1 In a 3½- or 4-quart slow cooker combine meat, beans, tomato sauce, undrained tomatoes, and frozen potatoes.

2 Cover and cook on low-heat setting for 8 to 10 hours or on high-heat setting for 4 to 5 hours.

Nutrition Facts per serving: 247 cal., 4 g total fat (1 g sat. fat), 45 mg chol., 634 mg sodium, 31 g carbo., 6 g fiber, 23 g pro.
Daily Values: 14% vit. C, 4% calcium, 20% iron

Old-Fashioned Beef Stew

Purchase precut stew meat from the butcher. Or select a beef chuck or shoulder roast and cut it into ¾- to 1-inch cubes.

Prep: 15 minutes Cook: Low 8 hours, High 4 hours Makes: 4 main-dish servings (6 cups)

- 1 pound beef stew meat, cut into ¾- to 1-inch cubes
- 12 ounces small potatoes, peeled and quartered (about 2 cups)
- 4 medium carrots, cut into ½-inch pieces (2 cups)
- 1 10¾-ounce can condensed cream of potato soup
- ½ cup water
- 1 envelope (½ of a 2.2-ounce package) beefy onion soup mix

1 In a 3½- or 4-quart slow cooker combine meat, potatoes, and carrots. In a bowl stir together condensed soup, water, and soup mix. Pour soup mixture over meat and vegetables in cooker.

2 Cover and cook on low-heat setting for 8 to 9 hours or on high-heat setting for 4 to 4½ hours.

Nutrition Facts per serving: 298 cal., 7 g total fat (2 g sat. fat), 73 mg chol., 1,262 mg sodium, 31 g carbo., 3 g fiber, 28 g pro.
Daily Values: 309% vit. A, 23% vit. C, 4% calcium, 23% iron

Beef and Cabbage Stew

A can of your favorite beer gives this classic stew a zesty foundation. Use preshredded cabbage to keep prep time quick and simple.

Prep: 10 minutes Cook: Low 7 hours, High 3½ hours Makes: 4 main-dish servings (6 cups)

1 pound beef stew meat, cut into ¾- to 1-inch cubes
4 cups packaged shredded cabbage with carrot (coleslaw mix)
3 tablespoons quick-cooking tapioca
1 envelope (½ of a 2-ounce package) onion soup mix
3 cups water
1 12-ounce can beer

1 In a 3½- or 4-quart slow cooker place meat and cabbage with carrot. Sprinkle with tapioca and soup mix. Pour water and beer over all.

2 Cover and cook on low-heat setting for 7 to 8 hours or on high-heat setting for 3½ to 4 hours.

Nutrition Facts per serving: 242 cal., 4 g total fat (1 g sat. fat), 67 mg chol., 476 mg sodium, 19 g carbo., 2 g fiber, 26 g pro.
Daily Values: 2% vit. A, 38% vit. C, 5% calcium, 18% iron

Creamy Beef-and-Potato Stew

Few beef and potato stews are creamy, but this version is. And it will make you see stew in a new light. Top with a sprinkling of Parmesan, if you like.

Prep: 10 minutes Cook: Low 7 hours, High 3½ hours; plus 15 minutes on Low
Makes: 4 main-dish servings (7½ cups)

- 12 ounces boneless beef chuck, cut into ¾-inch pieces
- 1 16-ounce package frozen cut green beans
- 1 5- to 5½-ounce package dry au gratin potato mix
- ½ teaspoon dried thyme, crushed
- 3 cups water
- 1½ cups half-and-half or light cream
- Finely shredded Parmesan cheese (optional)

1 In a 3½- or 4-quart slow cooker combine the meat, frozen green beans, dried potatoes, sauce mix from potatoes, and thyme. Pour water over all.

2 Cover and cook on low-heat setting for 7 to 8 hours or on high-heat setting 3½ to 4 hours. If using high-heat setting, turn to low-heat setting. Stir in half-and-half. Cover and cook for 15 minutes more to heat through. Ladle stew into bowls. If desired, sprinkle with Parmesan cheese.

Nutrition Facts per serving: 373 cal., 15 g total fat (8 g sat. fat), 84 mg chol., 845 mg sodium, 39 g carbo., 5 g fiber, 26 g pro.
Daily Values: 21% vit. A, 35% vit. C, 26% calcium, 21% iron

Fruited Beef Stew

Luscious dried apricots, peaches, cherries, and the like impart a bit of sweetness to the savory beef, potatoes, and onions in this thick stew. Relish each spoonful.

Prep: 10 minutes Cook: Low 7 hours, High 3½ hours Makes: 6 main-dish servings (7½ cups)

1 pound beef stew meat, cut into ¾- to 1-inch cubes
1 16-ounce package frozen loose-pack stew vegetables, thawed (3 cups)
1 7-ounce package mixed dried fruit
2 tablespoons quick-cooking tapioca
2 14-ounce cans beef broth (3½ cups)

1 Place meat in a 3½- to 4½-quart slow cooker. Cut up large pieces of stew vegetables and fruit; add to meat in slow cooker. Sprinkle with tapioca. Pour beef broth over all.

2 Cover and cook on low-heat setting for 7 to 8 hours or on high-heat setting for 3½ to 4 hours.

Nutrition Facts per serving: 231 cal., 3 g total fat (1 g sat. fat), 45 mg chol., 546 mg sodium, 32 g carbo., 3 g fiber, 19 g pro.
Daily Values: 90% vit. A, 4% vit. C, 2% calcium, 16% iron

Sweet-and-Sour Beef Stew

Beef stew takes on an Asian dimension with the addition of bottled sweet-and-sour sauce. Start off the meal with purchased egg rolls.

Prep: 10 minutes Cook: Low 10 hours, High 5 hours Makes: 6 to 8 main-dish servings (8 cups)

- 1½ pounds beef stew meat, cut into ¾- to 1-inch pieces
- 1 16-ounce package frozen loose-pack stew vegetables (3 cups)
- 2 10¾-ounce cans condensed beefy mushroom soup
- ½ cup bottled sweet-and-sour sauce
- ½ cup water
- ⅛ to ¼ teaspoon cayenne pepper

1 In a 3½- or 4-quart slow cooker place meat and frozen vegetables. Stir in soup, sweet-and-sour sauce, water, and cayenne pepper.

2 Cover and cook on low-heat setting for 10 to 11 hours or on high-heat setting for 5 to 5½ hours.

Nutrition Facts per serving: 291 cal., 9 g total fat (3 g sat. fat), 62 mg chol., 1,019 mg sodium, 19 g carbo., 2 g fiber, 30 g pro.
Daily Values: 74% vit. A, 4% vit. C, 1% calcium, 16% iron

Simple Short Rib Stew

Here's a stick-to-your-ribs meal with a nifty twist. The sweetness of bottled plum or hoisin sauce takes the place of ordinary barbecue sauce.

Prep: 35 minutes Cook: Low 7 hours, High 3½ hours Makes: 6 main-dish servings (8 cups)

Nonstick cooking spray
2 pounds boneless beef short ribs, trimmed and cut into 1½-inch pieces
1 pound tiny new potatoes, halved
5 carrots, cut into 1-inch pieces
1 12-ounce jar beef gravy
½ cup bottled plum sauce or hoisin sauce

1 Lightly coat a 12-inch skillet with cooking spray; heat over medium heat. In hot skillet cook meat, half at a time, until brown. Drain off fat.

2 In a 3½- or 4-quart slow cooker place potatoes and carrots. Place meat on vegetables. In a bowl stir together gravy and bottled sauce; pour over meat and vegetables.

3 Cover and cook on low-heat setting for 7 to 8 hours or on high-heat setting for 3½ to 4 hours. Skim fat from surface of stew. Ladle into bowls.

Nutrition Facts per serving: 621 cal., 26 g total fat (11 g sat. fat), 173 mg chol., 670 mg sodium, 30 g carbo., 3 g fiber, 62 g pro.
Daily Values: 258% vit. A, 23% vit. C, 5% calcium, 45% iron

Pesto Meatball Stew

When winter has worn out its welcome and you're ready for spring but the temperatures won't oblige, let this innovative meatball stew warm you from the inside.

Prep: 10 minutes Cook: Low 5 hours, High 2½ hours Makes: 6 main-dish servings (about 7 cups)

- 1 16-ounce package frozen cooked Italian-style meatballs (32), thawed
- 2 14½-ounce cans Italian-style stewed tomatoes, undrained
- 1 15- to 19-ounce can white kidney (cannellini) beans, rinsed and drained
- ½ cup water
- ¼ cup purchased basil pesto
- ½ cup finely shredded Parmesan cheese (2 ounces)

1 In a 3½- or 4-quart slow cooker combine the meatballs, undrained tomatoes, beans, water, and pesto.

2 Cover and cook on low-heat setting for 5 to 7 hours or on high-heat setting for 2½ to 3½ hours. Ladle soup into bowls. Sprinkle with Parmesan cheese.

Nutrition Facts per serving: 408 cal., 27 g total fat (10 g sat. fat), 34 mg chol., 1,201 mg sodium, 24 g carbo., 6 g fiber, 17 g pro.
Daily Values: 14% vit. A, 4% vit. C, 21% calcium, 12% iron

Pioneer Bean Stew

This is true campsite fare. Sloppy joe flavor, two kinds of beans, and ground beef combine for a slow cooker classic that's hearty, thick, tangy, and tender. Plan an after-dinner hike.

Prep: 15 minutes Cook: Low 4 hours, High 2 hours Makes: 8 main-dish servings (9½ cups)

1½ pounds lean ground beef
4 or 5 slices bacon, chopped (4 ounces)
2 15½-ounce cans sloppy joe sauce
2 15-ounce cans red kidney beans, rinsed and drained
1 15-ounce can butter beans, rinsed and drained
2 cups water

1 In a large skillet cook the ground beef and chopped bacon until meat is no longer pink. Drain off fat.

2 In a 4- to 6-quart slow cooker combine the sloppy joe sauce, kidney beans, and butter beans. Stir in the ground beef mixture and water.

3 Cover and cook on low-heat setting for 4 to 6 hours or on high-heat setting for 2 to 3 hours.

Nutrition Facts per serving: 446 cal., 19 g total fat (7 g sat. fat), 66 mg chol., 1,692 mg sodium, 41 g carbo., 8 g fiber, 26 g pro.
Daily Values: 5% vit. C, 8% calcium, 28% iron

Taco Chili

It looks like chili but tastes like a taco. The hominy (or corn) contributes its light-colored texture and a subtle sweet flavor. For extra richness, top with cheese or a scoop of sour cream.

Prep: 20 minutes Cook: Low 4 hours, High 2 hours Makes: 4 to 6 main-dish servings (8 cups)

1 pound lean ground beef
2 15-ounce cans seasoned tomato sauce with diced tomatoes
1 15-ounce can chili beans with chili gravy
1 15-ounce can hominy or whole kernel corn, undrained
1 1.25 ounce package taco seasoning mix

1 In a large skillet cook ground meat until brown. Drain off fat.

2 In a 3½- or 4-quart slow cooker combine the meat, tomato sauce, beans with chili gravy, undrained hominy, and taco seasoning mix.

3 Cover and cook on low-heat setting for 4 to 6 hours or on high-heat setting for 2 to 3 hours.

Nutrition Facts per serving: 477 cal., 18 g total fat (6 g sat. fat), 71 mg chol., 1,998 mg sodium, 49 g carbo., 12 g fiber, 35 g pro.
Daily Values: 13% vit. A, 36% vit. C, 8% calcium, 28% iron

Pork and Black Bean Potage

Tender chunks of pork join fortifying black beans and lentils in this thick soup that's perfect to serve when chilly winds blow. Enjoy a crisp apple for dessert.

Prep: 20 minutes Cook: Low 8 hours, High 4 hours Makes: 4 main-dish servings (about 6 cups)

Nonstick cooking spray
2 19-ounce cans ready-to-serve black bean soup
12 ounces lean boneless pork shoulder, cut into ¾-inch cubes
½ cup dry lentils, rinsed and drained
1 cup packaged shredded carrot
1 cup water
2 tablespoons grated Parmesan cheese

1 Lightly coat a 3½- or 4-quart slow cooker with cooking spray. In the prepared cooker combine soup, meat, lentils, carrot, and water.

2 Cover and cook on low-heat setting for 8 to 10 hours or on high-heat setting for 4 to 5 hours. Ladle soup into bowls. Sprinkle with Parmesan cheese.

Nutrition Facts per serving: 418 cal., 8 g total fat (3 g sat. fat), 61 mg chol., 938 mg sodium, 50 g carbo., 19 g fiber, 34 g pro.
Daily Values: 176% vit. A, 8% vit. C, 13% calcium, 41% iron

Pork, Lentil, and Apple Soup

Put autumn's apple harvest to good use. Here the apples dissolve to help thicken and sweeten the beef broth. It's a nice way to reward yourself after a day of raking leaves.

Prep: 20 minutes Cook: Low 6 hours, High 3 hours Makes: 4 main-dish servings (6 cups)

Nonstick cooking spray
1 pound lean boneless pork, cut into ½-inch pieces
1 cup dry lentils, rinsed and drained
3 cooking apples, peeled, cored, and cut up
1 teaspoon dried marjoram, crushed
2 14-ounce cans beef broth (3½ cups)

1 Lightly coat a 12-inch skillet with cooking spray; heat over medium heat. In hot skillet cook meat until brown. Drain off fat.

2 Transfer meat to a 3½-quart slow cooker. Add the lentils, apples, and marjoram. Add beef broth; stir to mix.

3 Cover and cook on low-heat setting for 6 to 8 hours or on high-heat setting for 3 to 4 hours.

Nutrition Facts per serving: 384 cal., 6 g total fat (2 g sat. fat), 71 mg chol., 741 mg sodium, 44 g carbo., 17 g fiber, 39 g pro.
Daily Values: 2% vit. A, 12% vit. C, 5% calcium, 29% iron

Spicy Ham-and-Garbanzo Bean Soup

For a less spicy version, use regular vegetable juice in place of hot-style juice.

Prep: 15 minutes Cook: Low 7 hours, High 3½ hours
Makes: 6 main-dish servings (about 8 cups)

1½ cups cubed cooked ham (8 ounces)
1 15-ounce can garbanzo beans (chickpeas), rinsed and drained
2 cups sliced carrots
1 cup sliced celery
4 cups hot-style vegetable juice
1 cup water

1 In a 3½- to 4½-quart slow cooker combine ham, beans, carrots, and celery. Pour vegetable juice and water over all.

2 Cover and cook on low-heat setting for 7 to 9 hours or on high-heat setting for 3½ to 4½ hours.

Nutrition Facts per serving: 187 cal., 5 g total fat (1 g sat. fat), 22 mg chol., 1,272 mg sodium, 23 g carbo., 5 g fiber, 12 g pro.
Daily Values: 232% vit. A, 47% vit. C, 6% calcium, 10% iron

Ham and Spinach Soup

This brothy combination provides a nutritious dose of spinach. The soup is a great way to get your iron and vitamins A and C.

Prep: 10 minutes Cook: Low 8 hours, High 4 hours Makes: 4 main-dish servings (about 7½ cups)

- 1 1-pound package cubed cooked ham (3 cups)
- 2 cups purchased shredded carrot
- 1½ teaspoons dried oregano, crushed
- 3 14-ounce cans chicken broth or reduced-sodium chicken broth (5¼ cups)
- 1 6-ounce package baby spinach leaves (about 8 cups)

1 In a 3½- to 5-quart slow cooker combine ham, carrot, and oregano. Pour chicken broth over all.

2 Cover and cook on low-heat setting for 8 to 10 hours or on high-heat setting for 4 to 5 hours. Stir spinach into soup. Ladle soup into bowls.

Nutrition Facts per serving: 281 cal., 15 g total fat (5 g sat. fat), 65 mg chol., 2,859 mg sodium, 12 g carbo., 3 g fiber, 24 g pro. Daily Values: 336% vit. A, 26% vit. C, 7% calcium, 16% iron

Ham and Black Bean Salsa Soup with Lime

Top this zesty, meaty soup with spoonfuls of sour cream and pass lime wedges to squeeze over the top of individual servings.

Prep: 20 minutes Stand: 1 hour Cook: Low 11 hours, High 5½ hours
Makes: 6 main-dish servings (10 cups)

- 2¼ cups dry black beans (about 1 pound)
- 2 cups chopped cooked smoked ham (10 ounces)
- 1 cup chopped yellow and/or red sweet pepper
- 3½ cups water
- 1 16-ounce jar purchased lime garlic salsa
- Dairy sour cream (optional)
- Lime wedges (optional)

1 Rinse beans; place in a large saucepan. Add enough water to cover beans by 2 inches. Bring to boiling; reduce heat. Simmer, uncovered, for 10 minutes. Remove from heat. Cover; let stand about 1 hour. Drain and rinse beans.

2 In a 3½- or 4-quart slow cooker combine the beans, ham, sweet pepper, and the 3½ cups water.

3 Cover and cook on low-heat setting for 11 to 13 hours or on high-heat setting for 5½ to 6½ hours or until beans are tender. If desired, use a potato masher to mash beans slightly in the slow cooker. Stir salsa into soup. Ladle soup into bowls. If desired, serve with sour cream and lime wedges.

Nutrition Facts per serving: 341 cal., 4 g total fat (1 g sat. fat), 28 mg chol., 1,176 mg sodium, 49 g carbo., 12 g fiber, 29 g pro.
Daily Values: 6% vit. A, 93% vit. C, 12% calcium, 24% iron

Split Pea Plus Soup

If you're a split pea fan, prepare to be impressed. This attractive version refreshes the original with smoky sausage, diced tomatoes, and carrots.

Prep: 15 minutes Cook: Low 7 hours, High 3½ hours Makes: 6 main-dish servings (7½ cups)

3 cups water
2 11½-ounce cans condensed split pea with ham soup
1 14½-ounce can diced tomatoes with garlic and onion, undrained
8 ounces cooked smoked sausage, sliced
1 cup purchased shredded carrot

1 In a 3½- or 4-quart slow cooker combine water, soup, undrained tomatoes, sausage, and carrot.

2 Cover and cook on low-heat setting for 7 to 9 hours or on high-heat setting for 3½ to 4½ hours.

Nutrition Facts per serving: 330 cal., 16 g total fat (6 g sat. fat), 32 mg chol., 1,724 mg sodium, 30 g carbo., 3 g fiber, 18 g pro.
Daily Values: 110% vit. A, 14% vit. C, 4% calcium, 18% iron

German Potato Soup

Tangy sauerkraut and hearty mustard infuse an old-style goodness here. With a slice of rye and some Swiss or Jarlsberg cheese, this brothy soup becomes a hearty lunch.

Prep: 10 minutes Cook: Low 7 hours, High 3½ hours
Makes: 6 to 8 main-dish servings (about 9⅔ cups)

- 1 pound cooked smoked sausage, halved lengthwise and cut into ½-inch slices
- ½ of a 28-ounce package frozen loose-pack diced hash brown potatoes with onion and peppers (about 4 cups)
- 1 16-ounce jar sauerkraut, rinsed and drained
- 2 tablespoons stone ground mustard
- 3 14-ounce cans chicken broth or reduced-sodium chicken broth (5¼ cups)

1 In a 4- to 5½-quart slow cooker place sausage, potatoes, sauerkraut, and mustard. Pour broth over all.

2 Cover and cook on low-heat setting for 7 to 9 hours or on high-heat setting for 3½ to 4½ hours.

Nutrition Facts per serving: 371 cal., 26 g total fat (9 g sat. fat), 51 mg chol., 3,860 mg sodium, 13 g carbo., 6 g fiber, 20 g pro.
Daily Values: 15% vit. C, 3% calcium, 7% iron

Black Bean and Kielbasa Soup

For a full-flavored meal that's pretty too, toss together slices of smoked Polish sausage (sometimes called kielbasa), bright yellow corn, and cans of black bean soup.

Prep: 15 minutes Cook: Low 6 hours, High 3 hours Makes: 6 main-dish servings (8 cups)

2 19-ounce cans ready-to-serve black bean soup
1 14½-ounce can diced tomatoes with garlic and onion, undrained
1 pound cooked, smoked Polish sausage, halved lengthwise and cut into ½-inch slices
1 cup frozen whole kernel corn

1 In a 3½- to 4½-quart slow cooker stir together the soup, undrained tomatoes, sausage, and corn.

2 Cover and cook on low-heat setting for 6 to 8 hours or on high-heat setting for 3 to 4 hours.

Nutrition Facts per serving: 425 cal., 24 g total fat (11 g sat. fat), 55 mg chol., 1,487 mg sodium, 34 g carbo., 8 g fiber, 17 g pro. Daily Values: 3% vit. A, 14% vit. C, 5% calcium, 25% iron

Sausage and Chicken Gumbo

Spicy, smoky gumbo gets its gumption from a hit of cayenne pepper. No need to prepare rice separately—it's already in the canned soup.

Prep: 10 minutes Cook: Low 6 hours, High 3 hours Makes: 6 main-dish servings (9 cups)

- 12 ounces cooked smoked sausage, halved lengthwise and cut into ½-inch slices
- 12 ounces skinless, boneless chicken thighs, cut into 1-inch pieces
- 1 16-ounce package frozen cut okra
- 2 10½-ounce cans or one 26-ounce can condensed chicken with rice soup
- 2 cups water
- ¼ teaspoon cayenne pepper

1. In a 3½- or 4-quart slow cooker place the sausage, chicken, and frozen okra. Pour the soup and water over all. Stir in the cayenne pepper.

2. Cover and cook on low-heat setting for 6 to 8 hours or on high-heat setting for 3 to 4 hours.

Nutrition Facts per serving: 362 cal., 22 g total fat (7 g sat. fat), 90 mg chol., 1,591 mg sodium, 12 g carbo., 3 g fiber, 28 g pro. Daily Values: 14% vit. A, 8% vit. C, 9% calcium, 10% iron

Easy Burgoo

Classic burgoo, a thick stew of various meats, includes whatever the hunter catches that day. This version mixes pork and chicken with cayenne pepper for sass.

Prep: 15 minutes Cook: Low 4 hours, High 2 hours Makes: 6 main-dish servings (8½ cups)

Nonstick cooking spray
1¼ pounds lean boneless pork, cut into ¾-inch pieces
2 10¾-ounce cans condensed chicken gumbo soup
1 16-ounce package frozen succotash, thawed*
2 cups frozen loose-pack diced hash brown potatoes with onion and peppers
2 cups water
¼ teaspoon cayenne pepper

1 Lightly coat a large skillet with cooking spray; heat over medium heat. In hot skillet cook meat, half at a time, until brown. Drain off fat.

2 In a 3½- or 4-quart slow cooker combine meat, soup, succotash, frozen potatoes, water, and cayenne pepper.

3 Cover and cook on low-heat setting for 4 to 6 hours or on high-heat setting for 2 to 3 hours.

***Note:** *You can substitute one 10-ounce package frozen lima beans, thawed, and 1 cup frozen whole kernel corn, thawed, for the succotash.*

Nutrition Facts per serving: 310 cal., 8 g total fat (3 g sat. fat), 57 mg chol., 994 mg sodium, 32 g carbo., 5 g fiber, 28 g pro.
Daily Values: 13% vit. A, 35% vit. C, 61% calcium, 2% iron

Pork and Mushroom Stew

This stew's light sage-infused sauce makes it an elegant early afternoon or evening meal. Ladle it over rice, egg noodles, or your favorite fluffy mashed potatoes.

Prep: 25 minutes Cook: Low 6 hours, High 3 hours
Makes: 4 to 6 main-dish servings (about 7 cups)

- Nonstick cooking spray
- 1½ pounds lean boneless pork, cut into ¾-inch pieces
- 1 16-ounce package frozen small whole onions, thawed
- 12 ounces whole mushrooms, quartered
- 1 10¾-ounce can condensed cream of mushroom soup with roasted garlic
- ½ teaspoon ground sage

1. Lightly coat a 12-inch skillet with cooking spray; heat over medium heat. In hot skillet cook meat, half at a time, until brown.

2. Place meat in a 3½- or 4-quart slow cooker. Add onions and mushrooms. In a bowl stir together soup and sage. Stir soup mixture into pork mixture in cooker.

3. Cover and cook on low-heat setting for 6 to 7 hours or on high-heat setting for 3 to 3½ hours.

Nutrition Facts per serving: 317 cal., 10 g total fat (3 g sat. fat), 103 mg chol., 645 mg sodium, 19 g carbo., 4 g fiber, 38 g pro.
Daily Values: 1% vit. A, 20% vit. C, 7% calcium, 20% iron

German-Style Pork Stew

Tender meat and potatoes nestle in a mushroom gravy flavored with just enough apple juice and caraway seeds—classic complements to pork. Serve apple pie for dessert.

Prep: 25 minutes Cook: Low 7 hours, High 3 ½ hours Makes: 4 main-dish servings (8 cups)

Nonstick cooking spray
2 to 2¼ pounds boneless pork shoulder or beef chuck, trimmed and cut into ¾-inch cubes
1 16- to 20-ounce package refrigerated diced potatoes
2 12-ounce jars mushroom gravy
1½ cups apple juice
2 teaspoons caraway seeds

1 Lightly coat a 12-inch skillet with cooking spray; heat over medium heat. In hot skillet cook and stir meat until light brown. Drain off fat.

2 In a 3½- or 4-quart slow cooker stir together pork, refrigerated potatoes, gravy, apple juice, and caraway seeds.

3 Cover and cook on low-heat setting for 7 to 8 hours or on high-heat setting for 3½ to 4 hours.

Nutrition Facts per serving: 462 cal., 16 g total fat (5 g sat. fat), 101 mg chol., 1,150 mg sodium, 44 g carbo., 3 g fiber, 34 g pro.
Daily Values: 15% vit. C, 6% calcium, 19% iron

Pork and Winter Squash Stew

Here versatile pork pairs with golden squash for a sage-scented stew. Serve over noodles or rice, and set out sliced pears with pecans for dessert.

Prep: 20 minutes Cook: Low 6 hours, High 3 hours Makes: 6 main-dish servings (7 cups)

- 2½ pounds boneless pork shoulder
- Nonstick cooking spray
- 1½ pounds winter squash (such as butternut), peeled, seeded, and cut into 1½- to 2-inch pieces
- 2 tablespoons quick-cooking tapioca
- 1 teaspoon ground sage
- 1 10½-ounce can condensed French onion soup
- ½ cup water
- Hot cooked noodles or rice (optional)

1 Trim fat from meat; cut meat into 1-inch cubes. Lightly coat a large skillet with cooking spray; heat over medium heat. In hot skillet cook meat, half at a time, until brown. Drain off fat.

2 Place squash in a 3½- or 4-quart slow cooker. Sprinkle with tapioca and sage. Add pork. Pour soup and water over all.

3 Cover and cook on low-heat setting for 6 to 8 hours or on high-heat setting for 3 to 4 hours. If desired, serve with hot cooked noodles.

Nutrition Facts per serving: 346 cal., 12 g total fat (4 g sat. fat), 123 mg chol., 565 mg sodium, 19 g carbo., 0 g fiber, 39 g pro.
Daily Values: 141% vit. A, 32% vit. C, 7% calcium, 17% iron

Tuscan Bean and Sausage Stew

In a pinch, you could mix and heat this stew on the stove top, but it's the extended cooking time that gives flavors a chance to meld into a luscious, tasty stew.

Prep: 15 minutes Cook: Low 6 hours, High 3 hours Makes: 6 main-dish servings (8 cups)

- 1 pound cooked smoked sausage, sliced
- 2 19- to 20-ounce cans or jars ready-to-serve Italian vegetable soup or hearty minestrone
- 1 15-ounce can white kidney (cannellini) beans, rinsed and drained
- 1 14½-ounce can Italian-style stewed tomatoes, undrained
- ¼ cup grated Parmesan cheese (1 ounce)

1 In a 3½- to 4½-quart slow cooker combine the sausage, soup, beans, and undrained tomatoes.

2 Cover and cook on low-heat setting for 6 to 8 hours or on high-heat setting for 3 to 4 hours. Ladle soup into bowls. Sprinkle with Parmesan cheese.

Nutrition Facts per serving: 516 cal., 28 g total fat (10 g sat. fat), 58 mg chol., 2,008 mg sodium, 37 g carbo., 8 g fiber, 28 g pro.
Daily Values: 67% vit. A, 11% vit. C, 17% calcium, 21% iron

Texas Two-Step Stew

Wake your taste buds with this lively stew that's great served with warm flour tortillas and lime wedges on the side. A topper of sour cream is a nice touch.

Prep: 20 minutes Cook: Low 4 hours, High 2 hours; plus 1 hour on Low or 45 minutes on High
Makes: 6 main-dish servings (10 cups)

8 ounces uncooked chorizo sausage
½ cup chopped onion (1 medium)
1 15-ounce can Mexican-style or Tex-Mex-style chili beans, undrained
1 15-ounce can hominy or one 11-ounce can whole kernel corn with sweet peppers, drained
1 6-ounce package regular Spanish-style rice mix
6 cups water

1 Remove casings from sausage, if present. In a medium skillet cook sausage and onion over medium heat until sausage is no longer pink. Drain off fat.

2 Transfer sausage mixture to a 3½- or 4-quart slow cooker. Stir in undrained chili beans, hominy, and the seasoning packet contents from the rice mix, if present (set aside remaining rice mix). Pour water over all.

3 Cover and cook on low-heat setting for 4 to 6 hours or on high-heat setting for 2 to 3 hours. Stir in remaining rice mix. Cover and cook on low-heat setting for 1 hour more or on high-heat setting for 45 minutes more.

Nutrition Facts per serving: 383 cal., 16 g total fat (6 g sat. fat), 33 mg chol., 1,385 mg sodium, 44 g carbo., 6 g fiber, 16 g pro.
Daily Values: 4% vit. A, 9% vit. C, 5% calcium, 16% iron

Potato and Bratwurst Stew

Imagine brats without the bun! Slices of tasty bratwurst enliven this chowderlike potato soup, while celery gives it a pleasing crunch.

Prep: 15 minutes Cook: Low 7 hours, High 3½ hours Makes: 6 main-dish servings (8 cups)

- 3 cups water
- 1 10¾-ounce can condensed cream of chicken with herb soup
- 1 pound cooked bratwurst, halved lengthwise and cut into ½-inch slices
- 1 20-ounce package refrigerated diced potatoes with onion
- 1½ cups sliced celery
- ¼ teaspoon salt
- ⅛ teaspoon black pepper

1. In a 3½- or 4-quart slow cooker stir together water and soup. Stir in the bratwurst, refrigerated potatoes, celery, salt, and pepper.

2. Cover and cook on low-heat setting for 7 to 8 hours or on high-heat setting for 3½ to 4 hours.

Nutrition Facts per serving: 352 cal., 21 g total fat (8 g sat. fat), 50 mg chol., 1,100 mg sodium, 26 g carbo., 3 g fiber, 14 g pro.
Daily Values: 5% vit. A, 20% vit. C, 5% calcium, 9% iron

Italian Sausage Stew

This one warrants a visit to your favorite Italian grocer. Pick up some choice sausage for this hearty stew made soft and rich with the addition of tortellini and cannellini beans.

Prep: 15 minutes Cook: Low 5 hours, High 2½ hours; plus 30 minutes on Low or 15 minutes on High
Makes: 6 main-dish servings (8½ cups)

1 pound Italian sausage
2 14-ounce cans seasoned chicken broth with Italian herbs (3½ cups)
1 15- to 19-ounce can white kidney (cannellini) beans, rinsed and drained
1 14½-ounce can diced tomatoes with basil, oregano, and garlic, undrained
1 9-ounce package refrigerated cheese-filled tortellini
Finely shredded Parmesan cheese (optional)

1 In a large skillet cook sausage over medium heat until brown. Drain off fat.

2 In a 3½- to 4½-quart slow cooker combine cooked sausage, broth, beans, and undrained tomatoes.

3 Cover and cook on low-heat setting for 5 to 6 hours or on high-heat setting for 2½ to 3 hours. Stir in pasta. Cover and cook on low-heat setting for 30 minutes more or on high-heat setting for 15 minutes more. Ladle soup into bowls. If desired, sprinkle with Parmesan cheese.

Nutrition Facts per serving: 441 cal., 20 g total fat (8 g sat. fat), 72 mg chol., 1,597 mg sodium, 40 g carbo., 5 g fiber, 24 g pro.
Daily Values: 11% vit. A, 9% vit. C, 16% calcium, 20% iron

Sausage and Sauerkraut Stew

Caraway seeds get credit for the nutty-sweet flavor of this saucy stew. And you don't have to add them to your shopping list because they're part of the canned sauerkraut.

Prep: 20 minutes Cook: Low 7 hours, High 3½ hours Makes: 4 to 5 main-dish servings (7½ cups)

12 ounces tiny new potatoes, quartered
2 cups packaged, peeled baby carrots, quartered
12 ounces cooked, smoked Polish sausage, cut into ½-inch slices
1 14- to 15-ounce can Bavarian-style sauerkraut (with caraway seeds), rinsed and drained
1 10½-ounce can condensed French onion soup
1 cup water

1 In a 3½- or 4-quart slow cooker combine potatoes, carrots, and sausage. In a large bowl combine sauerkraut, soup, and water; pour over sausage and vegetables in cooker.

2 Cover and cook on low-heat setting for 7 to 9 hours or on high-heat setting for 3½ to 4½ hours. Skim off fat. Ladle stew into bowls.

Nutrition Facts per serving: 469 cal., 27 g total fat (12 g sat. fat), 39 mg chol., 3,875 mg sodium, 43 g carbo., 4 g fiber, 14 g pro.
Daily Values: 341% vit. A, 41% vit. C, 4% calcium, 10% iron

Lamb Korma

The flavors of India emerge when you mix lamb, potatoes, and tomatoes with garam masala. You'll find garam masala at ethnic grocers and most supermarkets.

Prep: 15 minutes Cook: Low 8 hours, High 4 hours Makes: 6 main-dish servings (6½ cups)

- 2 pounds lean boneless lamb, cut into 1-inch cubes
- 1 tablespoon garam masala
- 3 cups cubed, peeled potatoes
- ¼ teaspoon each salt and black pepper
- 1 14½-ounce can diced tomatoes with garlic and onion, undrained
- ¼ cup water
- ¾ cup plain yogurt (optional)

1 In a bowl toss lamb with garam masala. Place potatoes in a 3½- or 4-quart slow cooker. Add seasoned meat. Sprinkle with salt and pepper. Pour undrained tomatoes and water over all.

2 Cover and cook on low-heat setting for 8 to 10 hours or on high-heat setting for 4 to 5 hours. Ladle stew into bowls. If desired, top with yogurt.

Nutrition Facts per serving: 282 cal., 8 g total fat (3 g sat. fat), 97 mg chol., 538 mg sodium, 18 g carbo., 1 g fiber, 33 g pro.
Daily Values: 32% vit. C, 4% calcium, 23% iron

North African Lamb Stew

Mango chutney weaves its velvety sweet-sour flavor throughout this thick brown stew. For a mellow accompaniment, ladle it over couscous.

Prep: 20 minutes Cook: Low 8 hours, High 4 hours Makes: 4 to 6 main-dish servings (6½ cups)

Nonstick cooking spray
2¾ pounds boneless lamb shoulder, trimmed of fat and cut into ¾- to 1-inch pieces
1½ cups thinly sliced carrots
1 cup sliced celery
2 cups water
1 9-ounce jar mango chutney (¾ cup)
2 tablespoons quick-cooking tapioca
Hot cooked couscous (optional)

1 Lightly coat a 12-inch skillet with cooking spray; heat over medium heat. In hot skillet cook meat until light brown. Drain off fat.

2 In a 3½-quart slow cooker place the carrots and celery. Add the meat. In a medium bowl combine the water, chutney, and tapioca; pour over the meat and vegetables.

3 Cover and cook on low-heat setting for 8 to 10 hours or on high-heat setting for 4 to 5 hours. If desired, serve over hot cooked couscous.

Nutrition Facts per serving: 569 cal., 19 g total fat (6 g sat. fat), 204 mg chol., 411 mg sodium, 35 g carbo., 3 g fiber, 62 g pro.
Daily Values: 265% vit. A, 33% vit. C, 9% calcium, 34% iron

Chicken and Wild Rice Soup

Orange shreds of carrot brighten this luscious soup that's loaded with tender chicken and nutty rice. You can add a tablespoon or two of white wine before serving.

Prep: 15 minutes Cook: Low 7 hours, High 3½ hours Makes: 6 main-dish servings (10½ cups)

Nonstick cooking spray
1 pound skinless, boneless chicken breasts, cut into ¾-inch pieces
1½ cups purchased shredded carrot
1 cup uncooked wild rice, rinsed and drained
3 14-ounce cans reduced-sodium chicken broth (5 cups)
2 10¾-ounce cans condensed cream of chicken with herb soup
1½ cups water

1 Lightly coat a large skillet with cooking spray; heat over medium heat. In hot skillet cook chicken until brown.

2 In a 4- to 5-quart slow cooker combine chicken, carrot, and rinsed and drained wild rice. Pour broth over all. Stir in soup and water.

3 Cover and cook on low-heat setting for 7 to 8 hours or on high-heat setting for 3½ to 4 hours.

Nutrition Facts per serving: 274 cal., 5 g total fat (2 g sat. fat), 52 mg chol., 1,321 mg sodium, 31 g carbo., 3 g fiber, 27 g pro.
Daily Values: 163% vit. A, 5% vit. C, 4% calcium, 8% iron

Creamy Cock-a-Leekie Soup

Leeks look like overgrown scallions, which makes sense because they're related to both the garlic and onion plant families. The leek's flavor, however, is more subtle than that of its relatives.

Prep: 15 minutes Cook: Low 5 hours, High 2½ hours Makes: 4 main-dish servings (6 cups)

Nonstick cooking spray
1½ pounds skinless, boneless chicken breast halves or thighs, cut into small pieces
2 10¾-ounce cans condensed cream of chicken with herb soup
2 cups water
6 medium leeks, sliced (2 cups)
1½ cups purchased shredded carrot
1 medium onion, cut into thin wedges

1. Lightly coat a 12-inch skillet with cooking spray; heat over medium-high heat. In hot skillet cook chicken until brown.

2. In a 3½- or 4-quart slow cooker stir together chicken, soup, water, leeks, carrot, and onion.

3. Cover and cook on low-heat setting for 5 to 6 hours or on high-heat setting for 2½ to 3 hours.

Nutrition Facts per serving: 348 cal., 8 g total fat (3 g sat. fat), 111 mg chol., 1,252 mg sodium, 24 g carbo., 4 g fiber, 45 g pro.
Daily Values: 245% vit. A, 17% vit. C, 9% calcium, 16% iron

Chicken-Vegetable Soup

You can count on basics like this old favorite to please time after time.

Prep: 15 minutes Cook: Low 7 hours, High 3½ hours Makes: 8 main-dish servings (12 cups)

1¼ pounds skinless, boneless chicken thighs, cut into ½- to ¾-inch pieces
2 14-ounce cans chicken broth (3½ cups)
2 10¾-ounce cans condensed cream of chicken with herb soup
1 16-ounce package frozen loose-pack broccoli, cauliflower, and carrots
1 20-ounce package refrigerated diced potatoes with onions

1 In a 4- to 6-quart slow cooker stir together chicken, broth, soup, frozen vegetables, and refrigerated potatoes.

2 Cover and cook on low-heat setting for 7 to 8 hours or on high-heat setting for 3½ to 4 hours.

Nutrition Facts per serving: 234 cal., 6 g total fat (2 g sat. fat), 63 mg chol., 1,238 mg sodium, 24 g carbo., 4 g fiber, 20 g pro.
Daily Values: 30% vit. A, 39% vit. C, 3% calcium, 8% iron

Chicken Cassoulet-Style Soup

This cassoulet features white beans and a variety of meats slow cooked so all flavors meld. Pasta sauce made with red wine and herbs adds a hearty depth.

Prep: 25 minutes Cook: Low 5 hours, High 2½ hours Makes: 6 main-dish servings (about 8 cups)

- 1 pound boneless, skinless chicken thighs, cut into ½-inch pieces
- 8 ounces smoked turkey sausage, cut into ½-inch slices
- 1 26-ounce jar pasta sauce with red wine and herbs
- 1 15- to 19-ounce can white kidney (cannellini) beans, rinsed and drained
- 1⅓ cups water
- 1 teaspoon dried oregano, crushed

1 In a 3½- or 4-quart slow cooker combine chicken, sausage, pasta sauce, beans, water, and oregano.

2 Cover and cook on low-heat setting for 5 to 7 hours or on high-heat setting for 2½ to 3½ hours.

Nutrition Facts per serving: 286 cal., 7 g total fat (2 g sat. fat), 88 mg chol., 1,178 mg sodium, 33 g carbo., 9 g fiber, 30 g pro.
Daily Values: 1% vit. A, 19% vit. C, 8% calcium, 20% iron

Mexican Chicken Soup

Chicken soup travels south of the border here, and it's packing plenty of flavor. Black beans and crushed tortilla chips provide the color and crunch.

Prep: 20 minutes Cook: Low 4 hours, High 2 hours Makes: 6 main-dish servings (8 cups)

- Nonstick cooking spray
- 1¼ pounds skinless, boneless chicken thighs or breast halves, cut into ½- to ¾-inch pieces
- 2 10¾-ounce cans condensed cream of chicken soup
- 2 cups water
- 1 15-ounce can black beans, rinsed and drained
- 1 14½-ounce can diced tomatoes and green chile peppers, undrained
- 1 teaspoon ground cumin
- Dairy sour cream (optional)
- Crushed tortilla chips (optional)

1 Lightly coat a large skillet with cooking spray; heat over medium heat. In hot skillet cook chicken, half at a time, until light brown. Transfer cooked chicken to a 3½- or 4-quart slow cooker.

2 In a bowl combine soup, water, beans, undrained tomatoes, and cumin. Pour over chicken in slow cooker.

3 Cover and cook on low-heat setting for 4 to 6 hours or on high-heat setting for 2 to 3 hours. Ladle soup into bowls. If desired, top with sour cream and sprinkle with crushed tortilla chips.

Nutrition Facts per serving: 310 cal., 11 g total fat (4 g sat. fat), 84 mg chol., 1,370 mg sodium, 26 g carbo., 6 g fiber, 29 g pro.
Daily Values: 18% vit. A, 17% vit. C, 8% calcium, 15% iron

Chicken Curry Soup

It's the coconut milk and curry powder that give this lush soup its exotic flair. Top it with chopped peanuts and toasted coconut, and serve it with wedges of pita bread.

Prep: 15 minutes Cook: Low 4 hours, High 2 hours; plus 15 minutes on Low
Makes: 6 main-dish servings (8⅓ cups)

- 1 10¾-ounce can condensed cream of chicken or celery soup
- 1 cup water
- 2 teaspoons curry powder
- 1¼ pounds skinless, boneless chicken thighs or breast halves, cut into ¾-inch pieces
- 2 cups sliced carrots
- 1 13½-ounce can unsweetened coconut milk
- Chopped peanuts (optional)
- Toasted coconut (optional)

1 In a 3½- or 4½-quart slow cooker combine soup and water. Stir in curry powder. Add the chicken and carrots to cooker. Stir to mix.

2 Cover and cook on low-heat setting for 4 to 5 hours or on high-heat setting for 2 to 2½ hours. If using high-heat setting, turn to low-heat setting. Stir in coconut milk. Cover and cook for 15 minutes more. Ladle soup into bowls. If desired, garnish with peanuts and/or coconut.

Nutrition Facts per serving: 302 cal., 19 g total fat (12 g sat. fat), 79 mg chol., 496 mg sodium, 11 g carbo., 1 g fiber, 22 g pro.
Daily Values: 206% vit. A, 9% vit. C, 3% calcium, 11% iron

Cheesy Cream of Chicken Soup

You'll crave this soup when there's a chill in the air. Good for a crowd that includes kids, it makes a nice addition to an after-game buffet.

Prep: 10 minutes Cook: Low 4 hours, High 2 hours; plus 30 minutes on High
Makes: 6 main-dish servings (9 cups)

- 1 pound skinless, boneless chicken thighs or breast halves, cut into ¾-inch pieces
- 2 10¾-ounce cans condensed cream of chicken soup
- 1 12-ounce can (1½ cups) evaporated milk
- 1 cup water
- 1 cup coarsely shredded carrot
- 1 5-ounce jar sharp process cheese spread

1 In a 3½- or 4-quart slow cooker combine chicken, soup, evaporated milk, water, and carrot. Stir to mix.

2 Cover and cook on low-heat setting for 4 to 5 hours or on high-heat setting for 2 to 2½ hours. If using low-heat setting, turn to high-heat setting. Stir in cheese spread. Cover and cook 30 minutes more or until cheese is melted.

Nutrition Facts per serving: 356 cal., 19 g total fat (9 g sat. fat), 103 mg chol., 1,179 mg sodium, 19 g carbo., 1 g fiber, 25 g pro.
Daily Values: 117% vit. A, 8% vit. C, 28% calcium, 7% iron

Asian Chicken Noodle Soup

Here's a light soup that's crowded with tender noodles and vegetables. A few drops of teriyaki sauce or soy sauce add another layer of flavor.

Prep: 15 minutes Cook: Low 5 hours, High 2½ hours; plus 10 minutes on High
Makes: 6 main-dish servings (9½ cups)

6 cups water
2 3-ounce packages chicken-flavored ramen noodles
1 teaspoon grated fresh ginger
2 cups chopped cooked chicken
1 16-ounce package frozen broccoli stir-fry vegetables
¼ cup sliced green onions (2)
Crushed red pepper (optional)
Teriyaki sauce or soy sauce (optional)

1 In a 3½- to 4½-quart slow cooker combine water, seasoning packets from noodles, and ginger. Add chicken and stir-fry vegetables.

2 Cover and cook on low-heat setting for 5 to 6 hours or on high-heat setting for 2½ to 3 hours.

3 If using low-heat setting, turn to high-heat setting. Stir in noodles. Cover and cook for 10 to 15 minutes more or until noodles are just tender. Stir in green onion. Ladle soup into bowls. If desired, sprinkle with crushed red pepper and serve with teriyaki sauce.

Nutrition Facts per serving: 180 cal., 1 g total fat (0 g sat. fat), 23 mg chol., 782 mg sodium, 26 g carbo., 2 g fiber, 15 g pro.
Daily Values: 14% vit. A, 19% vit. C, 3% calcium, 8% iron

Creamy Chicken Noodle Soup

Easy-to-make comfort foods never go out of style. When you're ready for a change, substitute 10 ounces frozen broccoli for the mixed vegetables.

Prep: 15 minutes Cook: Low 6 hours, High 3 hours; plus 20 minutes on High
Makes: 6 to 8 main-dish servings (10 cups)

- 2 10¾-ounce cans condensed creamy chicken mushroom soup
- 5 cups water
- 2 cups chopped cooked chicken
- 1 9- to 10-ounce package frozen mixed vegetables (cut green beans, corn, diced carrots, peas)
- 1 teaspoon seasoned pepper or garlic-pepper seasoning
- 1½ cups dried egg noodles

1 Place soup in a 3½- or 4-quart slow cooker. Gradually stir the water into the soup. Stir or whisk until smooth. Stir in cooked chicken, frozen vegetables, and seasoned pepper.

2 Cover and cook on low-heat setting for 6 to 8 hours or on high-heat setting for 3 to 4 hours.

3 If using low-heat setting, turn to high-heat setting. Stir in noodles. Cover and cook for 20 to 30 minutes more or until noodles are just tender.

Nutrition Facts per serving: 262 cal., 12 g total fat (3 g sat. fat), 63 mg chol., 908 mg sodium, 21 g carbo., 3 g fiber, 19 g pro.
Daily Values: 54% vit. A, 6% vit. C, 4% calcium, 9% iron

Chicken Chili Soup

Take this to a chili-tasting buffet if you want to stand out in the crowd. It'll score with those who love Southwestern flavors and spicy cumin. Spoon it over corn bread, if you like.

Prep: 15 minutes Cook: Low 7 hours, High 3½ hours Makes: 4 main-dish servings (7½ cups)

Nonstick cooking spray
1 9-ounce package frozen Southwestern seasoned cooked chicken breast strips, thawed and chopped
1 15- to 19-ounce can white kidney (cannellini) beans, rinsed and drained
1 16-ounce jar salsa
1 10¾-ounce can condensed cream of chicken soup
¼ to ½ teaspoon ground cumin
3 cups water

1 Lightly coat a 3½- or 4-quart slow cooker with cooking spray. In the prepared cooker combine the chicken, beans, salsa, soup, and cumin. Stir in water.

2 Cover and cook on low-heat setting for 7 to 8 hours or on high-heat setting for 3½ to 4 hours.

Nutrition Facts per serving: 346 cal., 8 g total fat (3 g sat. fat), 36 mg chol., 1,955 mg sodium, 46 g carbo., 7 g fiber, 21 g pro.
Daily Values: 21% vit. A, 29% vit. C, 10% calcium, 15% iron

Pepperoni Pizza Soup

This meal is a shoo-in with the kids: pizza soup ladled over a thick slice of garlic bread. The flavor is terrific, and it's a nice way to encourage pizza-loving kids to try new foods.

Prep: 10 minutes Cook: Low 4 hours, High 2 hours Makes: 6 side-dish servings (5½ cups)

- 1 14-ounce can beef broth (1¾ cups)
- 1 14- to 15-ounce can or jar pizza sauce
- 1¾ cups water
- 2 4-ounce cans sliced mushrooms, drained
- ½ of a 3½-ounce package sliced turkey pepperoni or pepperoni, cut up
- 6 slices frozen garlic bread

1. In a 3½- or 4-quart slow cooker combine the beef broth, pizza sauce, water, mushrooms, and pepperoni.

2. Cover and cook on low-heat setting for 4 to 6 hours or on high-heat setting for 2 to 3 hours.

3. To serve, prepare garlic bread according to package directions. Place a bread slice in each of 6 soup bowls; ladle soup over bread.

Nutrition Facts per serving: 168 cal., 7 g total fat (1 g sat. fat), 11 mg chol., 1,000 mg sodium, 20 g carbo., 2 g fiber, 7 g pro.
Daily Values: 3% vit. A, 7% vit. C, 2% calcium, 9% iron

Nacho Cheese-Chicken Chowder

Comforting flavor and a thick consistency make this a safe bet any night of the week. It's also a good way to lead a reluctant eater away from macaroni and cheese.

Prep: 10 minutes Cook: Low 4 hours, High 2 hours Makes: 6 main-dish servings (8 cups)

1 pound skinless, boneless chicken breast halves, cut into ½-inch pieces
2 14½-ounce cans Mexican-style stewed tomatoes, undrained
1 10¾-ounce can condensed nacho cheese soup
1 10-ounce package frozen whole kernel corn (2 cups)
Shredded taco or cheddar cheese

1 In a 3½- or 4-quart slow cooker stir together chicken, undrained tomatoes, soup, and corn.

2 Cover and cook on low-heat setting for 4 to 5 hours or on high-heat setting for 2 to 2½ hours. Ladle soup into bowls. Sprinkle with cheese.

Nutrition Facts per serving: 242 cal., 6 g total fat (3 g sat. fat), 55 mg chol., 644 mg sodium, 24 g carbo., 2 g fiber, 23 g pro. Daily Values: 24% vit. A, 8% vit. C, 12% calcium, 6% iron

Chicken-Corn Chowder

The vegetables are responsible for the pretty colors found here: bright yellow corn, red sweet pepper, and crunchy green celery.

Prep: 15 minutes Cook: Low 4 hours, High 2 hours Makes: 6 main-dish servings (7½ cups)

- 1 pound skinless, boneless chicken thighs, cut into ½- to ¾-inch pieces
- 2 10¾-ounce cans condensed cream of potato or cream of chicken soup
- 1 11-ounce can whole kernel corn with sweet peppers, undrained
- 1½ cups sliced celery
- 1 cup water
- 1 cup half-and-half or light cream

1. In a 3½- or 4½-quart slow cooker combine the chicken, soup, undrained corn, celery, and water.

2. Cover and cook on low-heat setting for 4 to 6 hours or on high-heat setting for 2 to 3 hours. Stir in half-and-half.

Nutrition Facts per serving: 261 cal., 10 g total fat (5 g sat. fat), 86 mg chol., 1,029 mg sodium, 24 g carbo., 3 g fiber, 19 g pro. Daily Values: 7% vit. A, 14% vit. C, 8% calcium, 10% iron

Cheesy Chicken-Rice Chowder

The word "chowder" applies to any thick, chunky soup—and this one certainly meets those standards. The vegetables, rice, and chicken bits simmer in a creamy tomato-based chowder.

Prep: 10 minutes Cook: Low 5 hours, High 2½ hours Makes: 5 to 6 main-dish servings (7½ cups)

- 1 26-ounce can condensed chicken with rice soup
- 2 cups water
- 2 cups frozen loose-pack peas and carrots
- 1 14½-ounce can diced tomatoes with Italian herbs, undrained
- 4 ounces American cheese, shredded (1 cup)
- ½ cup half-and-half, light cream, or milk

1 In a 3½- or 4-quart slow cooker combine soup, water, frozen peas and carrots, and undrained tomatoes.

2 Cover and cook on low-heat setting for 5 to 6 hours or on high-heat setting for 2½ to 3 hours. Stir in cheese until melted. Stir in half-and-half.

Nutrition Facts per serving: 250 cal., 12 g total fat (7 g sat. fat), 39 mg chol., 1,577 mg sodium, 23 g carbo., 3 g fiber, 13 g pro.
Daily Values: 130% vit. A, 28% vit. C, 23% calcium, 11% iron

Corn and Sausage Chowder

The corn gives this vibrant soup color, but it's the sausage that brings home the flavor. Serve it in a bowl with crusty bread for dinner or in a cup with a sandwich for lunch.

Prep: 15 minutes Cook: Low 8 hours, High 4 hours Makes: 6 main-dish servings (about 9 cups)

- 1 pound cooked smoked turkey sausage, halved lengthwise and cut into ½-inch slices
- 3 cups frozen loose-pack diced hash brown potatoes with onion and peppers
- 2 medium carrots, coarsely chopped
- 2½ cups water
- 1 15- to 16½-ounce can cream-style corn
- 1 10¾-ounce can condensed golden mushroom soup
- Snipped fresh chives or parsley (optional)

1 In a 3½- to 5-quart slow cooker place sausage, frozen potatoes, and carrots. In a bowl combine water, corn, and soup. Pour over meat and vegetables in cooker.

2 Cover and cook on low-heat setting for 8 to 10 hours or on high-heat setting for 4 to 5 hours. Ladle soup into bowls. If desired, sprinkle with chives.

Nutrition Facts per serving: 238 cal., 8 g total fat (2 g sat. fat), 53 mg chol., 1,280 mg sodium, 28 g carbo., 2 g fiber, 15 g pro.
Daily Values: 58% vit. A, 38% vit. C, 2% calcium, 8% iron

Oriental-Style Chicken Stew

This slow-cooked version of a stir-fry comes together in hours rather than minutes, and it's even easier to make than a traditional stir-fry. The secret lies in a bottle of stir-fry sauce.

Prep: 15 minutes Cook: Low 7 hours, High 3½ hours Makes: 4 main-dish servings (6½ cups)

- 2 pounds skinless, boneless chicken thighs, cut into 1-inch pieces
- 1½ cups thinly sliced carrots
- 1 15-ounce can or jar straw mushrooms, drained
- 1 cup bottled sesame-ginger stir-fry sauce
- ½ cup water
- 4 teaspoons quick-cooking tapioca

1 In a 3½- or 4-quart slow cooker combine chicken, carrots, and mushrooms. In a small bowl stir together stir-fry sauce, water, and tapioca; stir into chicken mixture in cooker.

2 Cover and cook on low-heat setting for 7 to 8 hours or on high-heat setting for 3½ to 4 hours.

Nutrition Facts per serving: 393 cal., 9 g total fat (2 g sat. fat), 188 mg chol., 1,701 mg sodium, 25 g carbo., 4 g fiber, 49 g pro.
Daily Values: 233% vit. A, 15% vit. C, 5% calcium, 22% iron

Mexican Meatball Stew

Eat this hearty stew with a side of warm corn bread and a crisp salad.

Prep: 10 minutes Cook: Low 6 hours, High 3 hours Makes: 8 to 10 main-dish servings (11 cups)

- 2 14½-ounce cans Mexican-style stewed tomatoes, undrained
- 2 12-ounce packages frozen cooked turkey meatballs (24), thawed
- 1 15-ounce can black beans, rinsed and drained
- 1 14-ounce can chicken broth with roasted garlic
- 1 10-ounce package frozen corn, thawed

1. In a 4- to 5-quart slow cooker combine undrained tomatoes, meatballs, beans, chicken broth, and thawed corn.

2. Cover and cook on low-heat setting for 6 to 7 hours or on high-heat setting for 3 to 3½ hours.

Nutrition Facts per serving: 268 cal., 10 g total fat (3 g sat. fat), 66 mg chol., 1,328 mg sodium, 30 g carbo., 8 g fiber, 20 g pro.
Daily Values: 2% vit. A, 16% vit. C, 9% calcium, 15% iron

Teriyaki Chicken Stew

If you want to serve a veritable feast, stop by a Chinese restaurant for take-out egg rolls and pot stickers, and cook up some rice or serve with chow mein noodles.

Prep: 10 minutes Cook: Low 3 hours, High 2 hours; plus 15 minutes on Low
Makes: 4 main-dish servings (6 cups)

- 1 16-ounce package frozen loose-pack stir-fry vegetable blend
- 2 cups chopped cooked chicken
- 1 8-ounce can sliced water chestnuts, drained
- ¾ cup teriyaki stir-fry sauce
- ½ cup water
- 1 13½-ounce can unsweetened coconut milk
- ¼ cup chopped cashews (optional)

1 In a 3½- or 4-quart slow cooker combine the frozen vegetables, chicken, water chestnuts, teriyaki sauce, and water.

2 Cover and cook on low-heat setting for 3 to 4 hours or on high-heat setting for 2 to 2½ hours. If using high-heat setting, turn to low-heat setting. Stir in coconut milk. Cover and cook for 15 minutes more. Ladle soup into bowls. If desired, sprinkle with chopped cashews.

Nutrition Facts per serving: 391 cal., 23 g total fat (17 g sat. fat), 62 mg chol., 559 mg sodium, 24 g carbo., 4 g fiber, 26 g pro.
Daily Values: 31% vit. A, 47% vit. C, 2% calcium, 15% iron

Mexican-Style Fish Chowder

Chunks of cod or other white fish get a flavorful kick in a creamy, zesty chowder. Serve with a basket of blue corn tortilla chips and a cold Mexican beer.

Prep: 15 minutes Cook: Low 3 hours, High 1½ hours; plus 1 hour on High
Makes: 6 to 8 servings (10½ cups)

- Nonstick cooking spray
- 2 10¾-ounce cans condensed cream of celery soup
- 1 16- to 20-ounce package frozen whole kernel corn
- 1½ cups milk
- 1 pound cod or other white-fleshed fish fillets
- 2 14½-ounce cans Mexican-style stewed tomatoes, undrained

1 Lightly coat a 3½- or 4-quart slow cooker with cooking spray. In the prepared cooker combine soup, corn, and milk.

2 Cover and cook on low-heat setting for 3 to 4 hours or on high-heat setting for 1½ to 2 hours. If using low-heat setting, turn to high-heat setting.

3 Stir chowder. Place fish on top of the mixture in the cooker. Cover and cook for 1 hour more. Stir in undrained tomatoes.

Nutrition Facts per serving: 293 cal., 8 g total fat (3 g sat. fat), 39 mg chol., 1,296 mg sodium, 36 g carbo., 2 g fiber, 21 g pro.
Daily Values: 8% vit. A, 45% vit. C, 12% calcium, 7% iron

Creamy Clam Chowder

Instead of ordering out, declare clam chowder a Friday night tradition at your place. Fragrant dillweed gives this mild soup a spark of extra flavor.

Prep: 10 minutes Cook: Low 6 hours, High 3 hours; plus 1 hour on High
Makes: 6 main-dish servings (9 cups)

- 3 6½-ounce cans minced clams
- 3 medium potatoes, peeled and cut into bite-size pieces (3 cups)
- 1 10¾-ounce can condensed cream of onion soup
- ½ teaspoon dried dillweed
- 2 to 3 cups half-and-half or light cream

1 Drain clams, reserving liquid. Cover clams and chill in refrigerator until needed. If necessary, add water to reserved clam liquid to make 1¾ cups.

2 In a 3½- or 4-quart slow cooker combine the clam liquid and potatoes. Stir in soup and dillweed.

3 Cover and cook on low-heat setting for 6 to 8 hours or on high-heat setting for 3 to 4 hours. If using low-heat setting, turn to high-heat setting. Stir in clams and enough half-and-half to make desired consistency. Cover; cook for 1 hour more.

Nutrition Facts per serving: 330 cal., 13 g total fat (7 g sat. fat), 97 mg chol., 525 mg sodium, 24 g carbo., 1 g fiber, 28 g pro.
Daily Values: 20% vit. A, 49% vit. C, 19% calcium, 147% iron

Cheesy Potato-Bean Soup

The soup's name might bring misleading images to mind, but rest assured this is no standard cheese soup.

Prep: 10 minutes Cook: Low 6 hours, High 3 hours Makes: 6 main-dish servings (about 8 cups)

- 1 26-ounce can condensed cream of chicken soup
- 3 cups frozen loose-pack diced hash brown potatoes
- 1 15- to 19-ounce can white kidney (cannellini) beans, rinsed and drained
- 3 cups water
- ½ teaspoon fennel seeds, crushed
- 8 ounces process Swiss cheese slices, torn

1 In a 3½- or 4-quart slow cooker combine soup, hash brown potatoes, beans, water, and fennel seeds.

2 Cover and cook on low-heat setting for 6 to 8 hours or on high-heat setting for 3 to 4 hours. Stir in cheese until melted.

Nutrition Facts per serving: 402 cal., 19 g total fat (9 g sat. fat), 42 mg chol., 1,603 mg sodium, 41 g carbo., 5 g fiber, 17 g pro.
Daily Values: 16% vit. A, 14% vit. C, 35% calcium, 15% iron

Picadillo Soup

Your taste buds will dance between the sweet, spicy, and savory in this truly unique Mediterranean-style soup. Apples and raisins tango with olives over ground beef.

Prep: 10 minutes Cook: Low 7 hours, High 3½ hours Makes: 6 main-dish servings (8 cups)

- 2 15-ounce cans chili without beans
- 1 14½-ounce can Mexican-style stewed tomatoes, undrained
- 2 cups water
- 2 large cooking apples, peeled, cored, and coarsely chopped (2¼ cups)
- ½ cup golden raisins
- ½ teaspoon apple pie spice or pumpkin pie spice
- Sliced pitted ripe olives and/or chopped peanuts (optional)

1 In a 3½- or 4-quart slow cooker combine chili, undrained tomatoes, water, apples, raisins, and spice.

2 Cover and cook on low-heat setting for 7 to 8 hours or on high-heat setting for 3½ to 4 hours. Ladle soup into bowls. If desired, sprinkle with olives and/or nuts.

Nutrition Facts per serving: 374 cal., 21 g total fat (10 g sat. fat), 37 mg chol., 991 mg sodium, 31 g carbo., 2 g fiber, 16 g pro.
Daily Values: 5% vit. A, 21% vit. C, 8% calcium, 14% iron

Hearty Onion-Lentil Soup

A combination French onion and lentil soup, this tastes great ladled over melted cheese-topped toasts. It's a light but warming meal-in-a-bowl.

Prep: 20 minutes Cook: Low 6 hours, High 3 hours Makes: 6 main-dish servings (about 7 cups)

- 4 cups water
- 2 10½-ounce cans condensed French onion soup
- 2 cups sliced celery or carrots
- 1 cup dry lentils, rinsed and drained
- 6 ¾-inch slices country French bread, toasted
- 1 cup shredded Swiss or Gruyère cheese (4 ounces)

1 In a 3½- or 4-quart slow cooker combine water, soup, celery, and lentils.

2 Cover and cook on low heat setting for 6 to 8 hours or on high-heat setting for 3 to 4 hours.

3 Arrange toasted bread slices on a baking sheet and top each with some of the cheese. Broil 3 to 4 inches from the heat for 2 to 3 minutes or until cheese is light brown and bubbly. Place a slice of cheese-topped bread in each bowl and ladle soup over toast.

Nutrition Facts per serving: 345 cal., 9 g total fat (4 g sat. fat), 19 mg chol., 1,130 mg sodium, 48 g carbo., 12 g fiber, 20 g pro.
Daily Values: 4% vit. A, 10% vit. C, 26% calcium, 22% iron

Easy Vegetable Minestrone

Curly rotini and chunky green or yellow beans crowd into this red brothy soup. Hunks of chunky bread taste great dunked in the broth.

Prep: 10 minutes Cook: Low 6 hours, High 3 hours; plus 15 minutes on High
Makes: 4 to 6 main-dish servings (8½ cups)

- 2 9-ounce packages frozen cut green and/or wax yellow beans
- 2 teaspoons spicy pizza seasoning
- 2 14-ounce cans vegetable broth (3½ cups)
- 3 cups vegetable juice
- 1½ cups dried rotini pasta
- Grated Parmesan cheese (optional)

1 In a 3½- to 5-quart slow cooker place frozen beans. Sprinkle with pizza seasoning. Pour vegetable broth and vegetable juice over all.

2 Cover and cook on low-heat setting for 6 to 7 hours or on high-heat setting for 3 to 3½ hours.

3 If using low-heat setting, turn to high-heat setting. Stir in pasta. Cover and cook for 15 to 20 minutes more or until pasta is tender. Ladle soup into bowls. If desired, sprinkle with Parmesan cheese.

Nutrition Facts per serving: 201 cal., 2 g total fat (0 g sat. fat), 0 mg chol., 1,414 mg sodium, 42 g carbo., 6 g fiber, 9 g pro.
Daily Values: 57% vit. A, 106% vit. C, 9% calcium, 16% iron

Caldo con Queso

Slightly tart with a subtle zing, this rich soup is dotted with bits of tomato, potato, and green chile peppers. Serve it solo or with a grilled ham sandwich.

Prep: 10 minutes Cook: Low 4 hours, High 2 hours; plus 15 minutes on High
Makes: 4 main-dish servings (7 cups)

- 2 14½-ounce cans diced tomatoes, undrained
- 2 10¾-ounce cans condensed cream of potato soup
- 1 4½-ounce can diced green chile peppers, drained
- ½ cup water
- 1⅓ cups whipping cream
- 1 cup shredded Monterey Jack cheese, Chihuahua cheese, or queso fresco (4 ounces)

1 In a 3½- or 4-quart slow cooker combine undrained tomatoes, soup, chile peppers, and water.

2 Cover and cook on low-heat setting for 4 to 6 hours or on high-heat setting for 2 to 3 hours.

3 If using low-heat setting, turn to high-heat setting. Stir in whipping cream. Cover and cook for 15 minutes more. Ladle soup into bowls. Sprinkle with cheese.

Nutrition Facts per serving: 519 cal., 41 g total fat (25 g sat. fat), 142 mg chol., 1,845 mg sodium, 25 g carbo., 3 g fiber, 13 g pro.
Daily Values: 71% vit. A, 44% vit. C, 37% calcium, 32% iron

Tomato-Spinach Bisque

Some tomato soups are good enough to eat every night of the week, and this velvety bisque is one of them. Dried tomatoes, baby spinach, and cream add up to something delectable.

Prep: 15 minutes Cook: Low 7 hours, High 3½ hours Stand: 5 minutes
Makes: 10 side-dish servings (8 cups)

- 1 2.4-ounce envelope regular-size dry tomato with basil soup mix
- 2 14½-ounce cans diced tomatoes with Italian herbs, undrained
- ⅓ cup snipped dried tomatoes
- 3 cups water
- 1½ cups whipping cream
- 6 cups fresh baby spinach

1 In a 3½- or 4-quart slow cooker combine tomato soup mix, undrained diced tomatoes, dried tomatoes, and water.

2 Cover and cook on low-heat setting for 7 to 8 hours or on high-heat setting for 3½ to 4 hours. Stir in whipping cream and spinach. Cover and let stand about 5 minutes or until spinach is slightly wilted.

Nutrition Facts per serving: 186 cal., 14 g total fat (9 g sat. fat), 49 mg chol., 563 mg sodium, 13 g carbo., 3 g fiber, 3 g pro.
Daily Values: 34% vit. A, 28% vit. C, 8% calcium, 11% iron

Mexican Cauliflower and Broccoli Chowder

Filled with nutritious veggies, this cheesy chowder surprises with its kick of heat. Top with sliced green onions or chopped jalapeño peppers if you like extra zing.

Prep: 10 minutes Cook: Low 4 hours, High 2 hours Makes: 6 side-dish servings (8 cups)

- 2 10¾-ounce cans condensed fiesta nacho cheese soup
- 1 cup water
- 1 16-ounce package frozen broccoli and cauliflower, thawed
- 1 11-ounce can whole kernel corn with sweet peppers, drained
- 1 cup chopped roma tomatoes
- 1½ cups half-and-half or light cream
- ¼ cup sliced green onions and/or sliced jalapeño chile peppers (optional)

1 Place soup in a 3½- or 4-quart slow cooker. Whisk the water into the soup until smooth. Stir in broccoli and cauliflower and corn.

2 Cover and cook on low-heat setting for 4 to 5 hours or on high-heat setting for 2 to 2½ hours. Stir in chopped tomatoes and half-and-half. Ladle soup into bowls. If desired, top with green onion and/or jalapeño peppers.

Nutrition Facts per serving: 261 cal., 14 g total fat (8 g sat. fat), 35 mg chol., 913 mg sodium, 26 g carbo., 5 g fiber, 9 g pro.
Daily Values: 48% vit. A, 86% vit. C, 18% calcium, 8% iron

Garden Bounty Tomato Soup

Use your favorite flavorful beef broth for this bountiful soup. The bounty here is fresh veggies—tomatoes plus your choice of carrots, celery, sweet peppers, fennel, and onion.

Prep: 25 minutes Cook: Low 6 hours, High 3 hours Makes: 8 to 10 side-dish servings (9 cups)

- 2 pounds roma tomatoes, chopped
- 2 14-ounce cans beef broth (3½ cups)
- 2 cups finely chopped vegetables (carrot, celery, sweet pepper, fennel, onion)
- 1 6-ounce can tomato paste
- 1 to 2 teaspoons sugar

1 In a 3½- or 4-quart slow cooker combine tomatoes, beef broth, vegetables, tomato paste, and sugar.

2 Cover and cook on low-heat setting for 6 to 8 hours or on high-heat setting for 3 to 4 hours.

Nutrition Facts per serving: 61 cal., 1 g total fat (0 g sat. fat), 0 mg chol., 372 mg sodium, 12 g carbo., 3 g fiber, 3 g pro.
Daily Values: 52% vit. A, 49% vit. C, 1% calcium, 6% iron

Curried Pumpkin Soup

A terrific starter to an elegant dinner, this soup will fool your guests into thinking you spent the day over a hot stove. Only you need to know how easy it is to make.

Prep: 10 minutes Cook: Low 5 hours, High 2½ hours Makes: 6 side-dish servings (8⅔ cups)

- 3 14-ounce cans chicken broth (5¼ cups)
- 2 15-ounce cans pumpkin
- ¼ cup honey
- 2 teaspoons curry powder
- ⅓ to ½ cup whipping cream

1 In a 3½- or 4-quart slow cooker combine the chicken broth, pumpkin, honey, and curry powder.

2 Cover and cook on low-heat setting for 5 to 6 hours or on high-heat setting for 2½ to 3 hours. Stir in enough cream to make desired consistency.

Nutrition Facts per serving: 163 cal., 7 g total fat (4 g sat. fat), 18 mg chol., 840 mg sodium, 25 g carbo., 4 g fiber, 4 g pro.
Daily Values: 629% vit. A, 10% vit. C, 5% calcium, 12% iron

2

Recipes Featuring Chicken and Turkey

Chicken and Bean Burritos

You'll get a different tasting burrito each time you try a new blend of salsa. Experiment!

Prep: 5 minutes Cook: Low 5 hours, High 2½ hours Makes: 8 servings

- 2 pounds skinless, boneless chicken breast halves
- 1 15-ounce can pinto beans in chili sauce
- 1 16-ounce bottle (1⅔ cups) salsa with chipotle peppers
- 8 10-inch flour tortillas, warmed*
- 1½ cups shredded Monterey Jack cheese (6 ounces)
- Shredded lettuce, chopped tomato, and/or dairy sour cream (optional)

1 In a 3½-quart slow cooker place chicken and undrained beans. Pour salsa over chicken and beans.

2 Cover and cook on low-heat setting for 5 to 6 hours or on high-heat setting for 2½ to 3 hours.

3 Remove chicken breast halves from cooker. On a cutting board use 2 forks to shred chicken into bite-size pieces. Using a potato masher, mash beans slightly in slow cooker. Return chicken to cooker, stirring to mix.

4 Divide chicken mixture evenly among the warmed tortillas. Top with shredded cheese. Fold up bottom edge of each tortilla over filling. Fold in opposite sides just until they meet. Roll up from the bottom. If necessary, secure with wooden toothpicks. If desired, pass lettuce, tomato, and/or sour cream.

***Note:** *To warm tortillas, stack tortillas and wrap tightly in foil. Heat in a 350°F oven about 10 minutes or until heated through.*

Nutrition Facts per serving: 400 cal., 12 g total fat (5 g sat. fat), 84 mg chol., 662 mg sodium, 34 g carbo., 5 g fiber, 38 g pro.
Daily Values: 11% vit. A, 16% vit. C, 25% calcium, 18% iron

Chicken Jambalaya

This rice with the flamboyant name—jambalaya—hails from New Orleans. The spicy Cajun flavor is sure to put zip in your day.

Prep: 15 minutes Cook: Low 5 hours, High 2½ hours; plus 45 minutes on High Makes: 6 servings

8 ounces skinless, boneless chicken breast halves
1 16-ounce package frozen loose-pack pepper stir-fry vegetables (yellow, green, and red sweet peppers and onions)
8 ounces smoked turkey sausage, halved lengthwise and cut into ½-inch slices
2 cups water
1 14½-ounce can diced tomatoes with jalapeño peppers, undrained
1 8-ounce package jambalaya rice mix

1 Cut chicken into ½-inch strips. Place stir-fry vegetables in a 3½- or 4-quart slow cooker. Top with chicken strips and turkey sausage. Add water, undrained tomatoes, and seasoning packet from rice, if present.

2 Cover and cook on low-heat setting for 5 to 6 hours or on high-heat setting for 2½ to 3 hours. Stir in rice mix. If cooking on low-heat setting, turn to high-heat setting. Cover and cook 45 minutes more or until most of the liquid is absorbed and rice is tender.

Nutrition Facts per serving: 265 cal., 4 g total fat (1 g sat. fat), 47 mg chol., 1,118 mg sodium, 37 g carbo., 2 g fiber, 19 g pro.
Daily Values: 14% vit. A, 13% vit. C, 4% calcium, 12% iron

Easy Chicken Rarebit

If you want to cut the cook time, brown the chicken slices in hot oil in a large skillet—you'll need to do two batches. Then plan on the shorter cooking time.

Prep: 25 minutes Cook: Low 4 hours, High 2 hours Makes: 6 servings

- 1¾ pounds skinless, boneless chicken breast halves
- 1 14- to 16-ounce jar cheddar cheese pasta sauce
- 1 tablespoon Worcestershire sauce
- 1 large onion, halved crosswise and thinly sliced
- 6 pumpernickel or rye buns, split and toasted, or 6 slices pumpernickel or rye bread, toasted and halved diagonally
- 4 slices bacon, crisp-cooked, drained, and crumbled (optional)
- 1 tomato, chopped (optional)

1 Cut chicken diagonally into ½-inch-thick slices; set aside. In a 3½- or 4-quart slow cooker stir together the pasta sauce and Worcestershire sauce. Add onion and chicken slices.

2 Cover and cook on low-heat setting for 4 to 5 hours or on high-heat setting for 2 to 2½ hours.

3 To serve, spoon chicken and sauce mixture over bun halves. If desired, sprinkle with crumbled bacon and tomato.

Nutrition Facts per serving: 340 cal., 12 g total fat (4 g sat. fat), 102 mg chol., 823 mg sodium, 21 g carbo., 3 g fiber, 36 g pro.
Daily Values: 5% vit. A, 5% vit. C, 12% calcium, 11% iron

Greek Chicken with Couscous

Some say the secret of good cooking is good ingredients. Here you'll find four Greek classics: chicken, feta, olives, and pine nuts.

Prep: 15 minutes Cook: Low 5 hours, High 2½ hours Stand: 5 minutes Makes: 8 servings

- 2 pounds skinless, boneless chicken breast halves
- 2 14½-ounce cans diced tomatoes with basil, oregano, and garlic, undrained
- 1½ cups water
- 2 6-ounce packages couscous with toasted pine nut mix
- 1 cup crumbled feta cheese (4 ounces)
- ½ cup pitted kalamata olives, coarsely chopped

1 Cut chicken into ½-inch pieces. Place chicken in a 3½- or 4-quart slow cooker. Pour undrained tomatoes and water over chicken.

2 Cover and cook on low-heat setting for 5 to 6 hours or on high-heat setting for 2½ to 3 hours. Stir in couscous. Cover and let stand for 5 minutes. Fluff couscous mixture with a fork.

3 To serve, spoon couscous mixture on each of 8 dinner plates. Sprinkle with feta cheese and olives.

Nutrition Facts per serving: 377 cal., 8 g total fat (4 g sat. fat), 82 mg chol., 1,226 mg sodium, 41 g carbo., 3 g fiber, 36 g pro.
Daily Values: 14% vit. A, 14% vit. C, 18% calcium, 17% iron

Sweet-and-Sour Chicken

Preparing this dinner may be less hassle than ordering takeout. To round out the meal, bake frozen egg roll appetizers and serve fortune cookies and sherbet for dessert.

Prep: 15 minutes Cook: Low 5 hours, High 2½ hours Makes: 4 servings

1 pound skinless, boneless chicken breast halves
2 9-ounce jars sweet-and-sour sauce
1 16-ounce package frozen loose-pack broccoli, carrots, and water chestnuts
2½ cups hot cooked rice
¼ cup toasted chopped almonds

1 Cut chicken into 1-inch pieces. In a 3½- or 4-quart slow cooker combine chicken, sweet-and-sour sauce, and frozen vegetables.

2 Cover and cook on low-heat setting for 5 to 5½ hours or on high-heat setting for 2½ to 2¾ hours. Serve with hot cooked rice. Sprinkle with almonds.

Nutrition Facts per serving: 477 cal., 6 g total fat (1 g sat. fat), 66 mg chol., 418 mg sodium, 71 g carbo., 4 g fiber, 32 g pro.
Daily Values: 56% vit. A, 36% vit. C, 5% calcium, 19% iron

Tex-Mex Chicken over Red Beans and Rice

Dressed up with colorful pepper strips, this full-flavored dish satisfies the desire for food that pleases the eye and palate.

Prep: 15 minutes Cook: Low 4 hours, High 2 hours Makes: 4 servings

- 1 pound skinless, boneless chicken breasts and/or thighs
- 1 16-ounce package frozen loose-pack pepper stir-fry vegetables (yellow, green, and red sweet peppers and onions)
- 1 12-ounce jar chicken gravy
- 1 cup bottled salsa with chipotles
- 1 7-ounce package red beans and rice mix

1 Cut chicken into bite-size strips. In a 3½- or 4-quart slow cooker combine the stir-fry vegetables, chicken strips, gravy, and salsa.

2 Cover and cook on low-heat setting for 4 to 5 hours or on high-heat setting for 2 to 2½ hours.

3 Cook red beans and rice according to package directions. To serve, divide red beans and rice among 4 shallow bowls. Using a slotted spoon, spoon chicken and vegetable mixture over the rice and beans.

Nutrition Facts per serving: 399 cal., 7 g total fat (2 g sat. fat), 68 mg chol., 1,480 mg sodium, 49 g carbo., 6 g fiber, 35 g pro.
Daily Values: 27% vit. A, 93% vit. C, 8% calcium, 20% iron

Chicken Stroganoff

Moist chicken, flavored mushroom soup, and sour cream spread across soft noodles. Stroganoff is classic comfort food.

Prep: 20 minutes Cook: Low 6 hours, High 3 hours Makes: 6 to 8 servings

- 2 pounds skinless, boneless chicken breast halves and/or thighs
- 1 cup chopped onion
- 2 10¾-ounce cans condensed cream of mushroom soup with roasted garlic
- ⅓ cup water
- 12 ounces dried wide egg noodles
- 1 8-ounce carton dairy sour cream
- Freshly ground black pepper (optional)

1 Cut chicken into 1-inch pieces. In a 3½- or 4-quart slow cooker combine the chicken pieces and onion. In a medium bowl stir together the soup and water. Pour over chicken and onion.

2 Cover and cook on low-heat setting for 6 to 7 hours or on high-heat setting for 3 to 3½ hours.

3 Cook noodles according to package directions. Drain. Just before serving, stir sour cream into mixture in cooker. To serve, spoon chicken mixture over hot cooked noodles. If desired, sprinkle with black pepper.

Nutrition Facts per serving: 532 cal., 14 g total fat (6 g sat. fat), 162 mg chol., 775 mg sodium, 54 g carbo., 3 g fiber, 46 g pro. Daily Values: 7% vit. A, 6% vit. C, 10% calcium, 17% iron

Thyme and Garlic Chicken Breasts

Thyme, garlic, a little orange juice, and a splash of balsamic vinegar flavor these moist, fork-tender chicken breasts.

Prep: 15 minutes Cook: Low 5 hours, High 2½ hours; plus 10 minutes on cooktop
Makes: 6 to 8 servings

- 6 cloves garlic, minced
- 1½ teaspoons dried thyme, crushed
- 3 to 4 pounds whole chicken breasts (with bone), halved and skinned
- ¼ cup orange juice
- 1 tablespoon balsamic vinegar

1. Sprinkle garlic and thyme over chicken. Place chicken pieces in a 3½- or 4-quart slow cooker. Pour orange juice and vinegar over chicken.

2. Cover and cook on low-heat setting for 5 to 6 hours or on high-heat setting for 2½ to 3 hours.

3. Remove chicken from cooker; cover and keep warm. Skim off fat from cooking juices. Strain juices into a saucepan. Bring to boiling; reduce heat. Boil gently, uncovered, 10 minutes or until reduced to 1 cup. Pass juices to spoon over chicken.

Nutrition Facts per serving: 178 cal., 2 g total fat (0 g sat. fat), 85 mg chol., 78 mg sodium, 3 g carbo., 0 g fiber, 34 g pro.
Daily Values: 2% vit. A, 13% vit. C, 3% calcium, 7% iron

Coq au Vin Stew

Never mind traditional pairings. Beefy onion soup mix and red wine combine with chicken for a succulent stew that's luscious on a cold night. Mop up every drop with bread.

Prep: 20 minutes Cook: Low 5 hours, High 2½ hours Makes: 4 servings

Nonstick cooking spray
3 pounds chicken thighs, skinned
1 envelope (½ of a 2.2-ounce package) beefy onion soup mix
1½ cups frozen small whole onions
2 cups fresh button or wild mushrooms, quartered
½ cup dry red wine

1 Lightly coat a large skillet with cooking spray; heat over medium heat. In hot skillet cook chicken thighs, in several batches, until brown on both sides. Drain off fat. Place chicken in a 3½- or 4-quart slow cooker.

2 Sprinkle chicken with soup mix. Add onions and mushrooms. Pour wine over all.

3 Cover and cook on low-heat setting for 5 to 6 hours or on high-heat setting for 2½ to 3 hours.

Nutrition Facts per serving: 305 cal., 8 g total fat (2 g sat. fat), 161 mg chol., 759 mg sodium, 12 g carbo., 2 g fiber, 41 g pro.
Daily Values: 2% vit. A, 14% vit. C, 8% calcium, 14% iron

Mediterranean Chicken

Turn this tender chicken entrée into a one-dish meal by serving it over polenta or couscous. Your family will clamor for seconds.

Prep: 20 minutes Cook: Low 6 hours, High 3 hours Makes: 6 servings

Nonstick cooking spray
2½ pounds chicken thighs and/or drumsticks, skinned
1 8- or 9-ounce package frozen artichoke hearts
¾ cup pitted kalamata olives
1 28-ounce jar roasted garlic pasta sauce
1 cup crumbled feta cheese (4 ounces)

1 Lightly coat a 3½- or 4-quart slow cooker with cooking spray. Place chicken pieces in the prepared cooker. Top with artichoke hearts and olives. Pour pasta sauce over artichokes and olives.

2 Cover and cook on low-heat setting for 6 to 7 hours or on high-heat setting for 3 to 3½ hours. To serve, sprinkle each serving with feta cheese.

**Nutrition Facts per serving: 296 cal., 13 g total fat (5 g sat. fat), 111 mg chol., 971 mg sodium, 16 g carbo., 4 g fiber, 28 g pro.
Daily Values: 13% vit. A, 18% vit. C, 22% calcium, 12% iron**

Honey-Mustard Chicken with Sweet Potatoes

Feel like something on the sweet side tonight? Indulge yourself with a medley of chicken, savory onions, and vitamin-rich sweet potatoes.

Prep: 20 minutes Cook: Low 7 hours, High 3½ hours Makes: 6 servings

- 6 medium sweet potatoes, peeled and quartered (about 2½ pounds)
- 1 small onion, cut into thin wedges
- 2 to 2½ pounds chicken thighs and/or drumsticks, skinned
- ¾ cup bottled honey-mustard salad dressing
- ½ teaspoon dried rosemary, crushed

1 In a 4½- to 6-quart slow cooker place sweet potatoes and onion wedges. Place chicken pieces on vegetables.

2 In a small bowl stir together salad dressing and rosemary. Pour over chicken.

3 Cover and cook on low-heat setting for 7 to 9 hours or on high-heat setting for 3½ to 4½ hours. Using a slotted spoon, transfer chicken and vegetables to a serving platter. Whisk cooking liquid until smooth; pass with chicken and vegetables.

Nutrition Facts per serving: 378 cal., 16 g total fat (2 g sat. fat), 71 mg chol., 186 mg sodium, 40 g carbo., 4 g fiber, 19 g pro.
Daily Values: 492% vit. A, 41% vit. C, 4% calcium, 9% iron

Gingered Chutney Chicken

Here's a mild sweet-sour chicken made with mango chutney and chili sauce. Serve jasmine rice alongside to complement the dish.

Prep: 20 minutes Cook: Low 5 hours, High 2½ hours Makes: 6 servings

- ½ cup mango chutney
- ¼ cup bottled chili sauce
- 2 tablespoons quick-cooking tapioca
- 1½ teaspoons grated fresh ginger or ½ teaspoon ground ginger
- 12 chicken thighs, skinned (about 4 pounds)

1 Cut up any large pieces of fruit in the chutney. In a 4- to 5-quart slow cooker combine chutney, chili sauce, tapioca, and ginger. Add chicken, turning to coat.

2 Cover and cook on low-heat setting for 5 to 6 hours or on high-heat setting for 2½ to 3 hours.

Nutrition Facts per serving: 264 cal., 7 g total fat (2 g sat. fat), 143 mg chol., 494 mg sodium, 16 g carbo., 1 g fiber, 34 g pro.
Daily Values: 11% vit. A, 17% vit. C, 2% calcium, 10% iron

Finger Lickin' Barbecue Chicken

This recipe's secrets come from unexpected sources: the hot dog stand (mustard) and the breakfast table (preserves).

Prep: 10 minutes Cook: Low 6 hours, High 3 hours Makes: 4 to 6 servings

- 2½ to 3 pounds chicken drumsticks, skinned if desired
- 1 cup bottled barbecue sauce
- ⅓ cup apricot or peach preserves
- 2 teaspoons yellow mustard

1 Place chicken in a 3½- or 4-quart slow cooker. In a small bowl stir together the barbecue sauce, preserves, and mustard. Pour over chicken.

2 Cover and cook on low-heat setting for 6 to 8 hours or on high-heat setting for 3 to 4 hours. Remove chicken to serving dish; cover and keep warm. If desired, transfer sauce from cooker to a medium saucepan. Bring to boiling; reduce heat. Simmer, uncovered, 10 minutes or until desired consistency. Pass sauce with chicken.

Nutrition Facts per serving: 456 cal., 17 g total fat (4 g sat. fat), 154 mg chol., 963 mg sodium, 37 g carbo., 2 g fiber, 38 g pro.
Daily Values: 5% vit. A, 15% vit. C, 5% calcium, 13% iron

Cherried Chicken

This fruity dish has a tasty blend of seasonings, and it's especially satisfying served over hot cooked rice or couscous.

Prep: 20 minutes Cook: Low 5 hours, High 2½ hours Makes: 4 servings

2½ to 3 pounds chicken drumsticks, skinned
1 teaspoon herb-pepper seasoning
1 15- to 17-ounce can pitted dark sweet cherries, drained
1 12-ounce bottle chili sauce
½ cup packed brown sugar

1 Sprinkle chicken evenly with herb-pepper seasoning. Place chicken in a 3½- or 4-quart slow cooker. In a bowl combine drained cherries, chili sauce, and brown sugar. Pour over chicken.

2 Cover and cook on low-heat setting for 5 to 6 hours or on high-heat setting for 2½ to 3 hours. Remove chicken to a serving platter. Skim fat from sauce. Spoon some sauce over chicken; pass remaining sauce.

Nutrition Facts per serving: 410 cal., 5 g total fat (1 g sat. fat), 105 mg chol., 1,539 mg sodium, 63 g carbo., 7 g fiber, 31 g pro.
Daily Values: 15% vit. A, 33% vit. C, 7% calcium, 17% iron

Homestyle Chicken and Stuffing

This is a great way to use up leftover chicken (or Thanksgiving turkey), but if you don't have any, thaw a package of frozen diced cooked chicken or cut up a deli-roasted chicken.

Prep: 15 minutes Cook: Low 5 hours, High 2½ hours Makes: 6 servings

1 10¾-ounce can reduced-fat and reduced-sodium condensed cream of chicken soup or cream of mushroom soup
¼ cup butter or margarine, melted
¼ cup water
1 16-ounce package frozen loose-pack broccoli, corn, and red sweet peppers
2½ cups cubed cooked chicken
1 8-ounce package corn bread stuffing mix

1 In a very large bowl stir together soup, butter, and water. Add frozen vegetables, chicken, and stuffing mix; stir until combined. Transfer mixture to a 3½- or 4-quart slow cooker.

2 Cover and cook on low-heat setting for 5 to 6 hours or on high-heat setting for 2½ to 3 hours.

Nutrition Facts per serving: 393 cal., 14 g total fat (6 g sat. fat), 76 mg chol., 1,041 mg sodium, 40 g carbo., 3 g fiber, 24 g pro.
Daily Values: 30% vit. A, 52% vit. C, 5% calcium, 11% iron

Chicken Tortilla Soup

Both chunky and crunchy, Chicken Tortilla Soup is always surprisingly good. Olé!

Prep: 15 minutes Cook: Low 6 hours, High 3 hours Makes: 4 servings

2 14-ounce cans chicken with roasted garlic broth
1 14½-ounce can Mexican-style stewed tomatoes, undrained
2 cups chopped cooked chicken
2 cups frozen loose-pack pepper stir-fry vegetables (yellow, green, and red sweet peppers and onions)
1 cup crushed tortilla chips with lime or tortilla chips
Dairy sour cream, snipped fresh cilantro, and/or chopped avocado (optional)

1 In a 3½- or 4-quart slow cooker combine broth, undrained tomatoes, chicken, and stir-fry vegetables.

2 Cover and cook on low-heat setting for 6 to 7 hours or on high-heat setting for 3 to 3½ hours.

3 To serve, ladle soup into warm bowls and top each serving with crushed tortilla chips. If desired, garnish with sour cream, cilantro, and/or avocado.

Nutrition Facts per serving: 181 cal., 4 g total fat (1 g sat. fat), 36 mg chol., 1,383 mg sodium, 19 g carbo., 1 g fiber, 18 g pro.
Daily Values: 9% vit. A, 51% vit. C, 3% calcium, 3% iron

Smoky Chicken and Cheesy Potato Casserole

Smoked chicken and cheese distinguish this creamy comfort food casserole.

Prep: 20 minutes Cook: Low 5 hours Makes: 6 servings

- Nonstick cooking spray
- 1 10¾-ounce can condensed cream of chicken with herbs soup
- 1 8-ounce carton dairy sour cream
- 6 ounces smoked cheddar cheese, shredded (1½ cups)
- 1 28-ounce package frozen loose-pack diced hash brown potatoes with onion and peppers, thawed
- 3 cups chopped smoked or roasted chicken or turkey
- Crushed croutons (optional)

1 Lightly coat a 3½- or 4-quart slow cooker with cooking spray. In the cooker combine soup, sour cream, cheese, potatoes, and chicken.

2 Cover and cook on low-heat setting for 5 to 6 hours. If desired, top each serving with crushed croutons.

**Nutrition Facts per serving: 399 cal., 20 g total fat (12 g sat. fat), 80 mg chol., 1,313 mg sodium, 31 g carbo., 3 g fiber, 25 g pro.
Daily Values: 20% vit. A, 25% vit. C, 27% calcium, 10% iron**

Sloppy Chicken Pizza Joes

Back off, ground beef—chicken can get sloppy too! And because joes are a kid-favorite, why not sneak in some healthful veggies?

Prep: 20 minutes Cook: Low 6 hours, High 3 hours Broil: 1 minute Makes: 8 sandwiches

- Nonstick cooking spray
- 3 pounds uncooked ground chicken or uncooked ground turkey
- 2 14-ounce jars pizza sauce
- 2 cups frozen loose-pack pepper stir-fry vegetables (yellow, green, and red sweet peppers and onions), thawed and chopped
- 8 hoagie buns, split
- 8 slices mozzarella or provolone cheese (8 ounces)

1 Coat a large skillet with cooking spray. Cook chicken in the skillet over medium-high heat until no longer pink and cooked through.

2 In a 3½- or 4-quart slow cooker stir together the pizza sauce and chopped vegetables. Stir in cooked chicken.

3 Cover and cook on low-heat setting for 6 to 8 hours or on high-heat setting for 3 to 4 hours.

4 Arrange split buns, cut sides up, on an unheated broiler pan. Broil 3 inches from the heat for 1 to 2 minutes or until toasted. Spoon meat mixture onto toasted roll bottoms. Top each with a slice of cheese and a bun top.

Nutrition Facts per sandwich: 641 cal., 24 g total fat (3 g sat. fat), 16 mg chol., 1,132 mg sodium, 58 g carbo., 2 g fiber, 47 g pro.
Daily Values: 6% vit. A, 21% vit. C, 29% calcium, 24% iron

Sesame-Ginger Turkey Wraps

This recipe makes enough for a crowd. Refrigerate any leftover filling for another meal, and the next time, try it on buns.

Prep: 20 minutes Cook: Low 6 hours, High 3 hours Stand: 5 minutes Makes: 12 servings

Nonstick cooking spray
3 turkey thighs, skinned (3½ to 4 pounds)
1 cup bottled sesame-ginger stir-fry sauce
¼ cup water
1 16-ounce package shredded broccoli (broccoli slaw mix)
12 8-inch flour tortillas, warmed*
¾ cup sliced green onions (6)

1 Lightly coat a 3½- or 4-quart slow cooker with cooking spray. Place turkey thighs in prepared cooker. In a small bowl stir together stir-fry sauce and water. Pour over turkey in cooker.

2 Cover and cook on low-heat setting for 6 to 7 hours or on high-heat setting for 3 to 3½ hours.

3 Remove turkey from slow cooker; cool slightly. Remove turkey meat from bones; discard bones. Using two forks, shred turkey into bite-size pieces. Place broccoli slaw mix in sauce in slow cooker. Stir to coat; cover and let stand for 5 minutes. Remove from cooker with a slotted spoon.

4 To assemble, place some of the shredded turkey on each warmed tortilla. Top with some of the broccoli mixture and green onions. Spoon some of the sauce from cooker on top of onions. Roll up and serve immediately.

***Note:** *To warm tortillas, stack tortillas and wrap tightly in foil. Heat in a 350°F oven about 10 minutes or until heated through.*

Nutrition Facts per serving: 207 cal., 5 g total fat (1 g sat. fat), 67 mg chol., 422 mg sodium, 20 g carbo., 2 g fiber, 20 g pro.
Daily Values: 25% vit. A, 57% vit. C, 6% calcium, 15% iron

Maple-Mustard-Sauced Turkey Thighs

Maple and mustard combine to form a succulent glaze for this tasty turkey dish. Use red-skinned potatoes for added color.

Prep: 20 minutes Cook: Low 6 hours, High 3 hours Makes: 4 servings

1 pound new potatoes, quartered
2 to 2½ pounds turkey thighs (about 2 thighs), skinned
⅓ cup coarse-grain brown mustard
¼ cup maple syrup or maple-flavored syrup
1 tablespoon quick-cooking tapioca

1 Place potatoes in a 3½- or 4-quart slow cooker. Place turkey thighs on potatoes. In a small bowl stir together mustard, syrup, and tapioca. Pour over turkey.

2 Cover and cook on low-heat setting for 6 to 7 hours or on high-heat setting for to 3 to 3½ hours.

Nutrition Facts per serving: 377 cal., 10 g total fat (3 g sat. fat), 93 mg chol., 369 mg sodium, 36 g carbo., 2 g fiber, 36 g pro.
Daily Values: 24% vit. C, 9% calcium, 26% iron

Cranberry-Sauced Turkey Thighs

The punch of cranberries joins the kick of chili sauce for a knockout combination. Mashed sweet or white potatoes will take the meal out for the count.

Prep: 10 minutes Cook: Low 9 hours, High 4½ hours Makes: 4 to 6 servings

- 1 16-ounce can jellied cranberry sauce
- ½ cup bottled chili sauce
- 1 tablespoon vinegar
- ¼ teaspoon pumpkin pie spice
- 2½ to 3 pounds turkey thighs (2 or 3 thighs), skinned

1 In a 3½- or 4-quart slow cooker stir together cranberry sauce, chili sauce, vinegar, and spice. Place turkey thighs, meaty side down, on sauce mixture.

2 Cover and cook on low-heat setting for 9 to 10 hours or on high-heat setting for 4½ to 5 hours.

3 Transfer turkey to a serving dish. Skim fat from sauce. Pass sauce with turkey.

Nutrition Facts per serving: 388 cal., 5 g total fat (2 g sat. fat), 145 mg chol., 300 mg sodium, 46 g carbo., 2 g fiber, 37 g pro.
Daily Values: 1% vit. A, 4% vit. C, 3% calcium, 20% iron

Turkey Shepherd's Pie

Traditionally made with lamb or mutton, shepherd's pie works equally well slow cooked with turkey and frozen vegetables. Dried thyme infuses an herbal note.

Prep: 20 minutes Cook: Low 6 hours, High 3 hours; plus 10 minutes on High Makes: 4 servings

- 12 ounces turkey breast tenderloin or skinless, boneless chicken breast halves
- 1 10-ounce package loose-pack frozen mixed vegetables
- 1 12-ounce jar turkey or chicken gravy
- 1 teaspoon dried thyme, crushed
- 1 20-ounce package refrigerated mashed potatoes

1 Cut turkey into ½-inch strips. In a 3½- or 4-quart slow cooker place vegetables. Top with turkey strips. In a bowl stir together gravy and thyme; pour over turkey.

2 Cover and cook on low-heat setting for 6 to 7 hours or on high-heat setting for 3 to 3½ hours. If cooking on low-heat setting, turn to high-heat setting.

3 Using a spoon, drop mashed potatoes into 8 small mounds on top of turkey mixture. Cover and cook for 10 minutes more. To serve, in each of 4 shallow bowls spoon some of the turkey mixture and two of the potato mounds.

Nutrition Facts per serving: 297 cal., 5 g total fat (1 g sat. fat), 51 mg chol., 781 mg sodium, 33 g carbo., 4 g fiber, 27 g pro.
Daily Values: 74% vit. A, 54% vit. C, 5% calcium, 15% iron

Turkey and Pasta Primavera

This is a delightful meal that serves all the family gathered for Sunday dinner. A sprinkling of Parmesan cheese lends a sharp note to the creamy blend.

Prep: 15 minutes Cook: Low 4 hours, High 2 hours Makes: 8 servings

- 2 pounds turkey breast tenderloins or skinless, boneless chicken breast halves
- 1 16-ounce package frozen loose-pack sugar snap stir-fry vegetables (sugar snap peas, carrots, onions, and mushrooms)
- 2 teaspoons dried basil, oregano, or Italian seasoning, crushed
- 1 16-ounce jar Alfredo pasta sauce
- 12 ounces dried spaghetti or linguine, broken
- Shredded Parmesan cheese (optional)

1 Cut turkey into 1-inch pieces. In a 4½- to 6-quart slow cooker combine turkey and vegetables. Sprinkle with dried herb. Stir in Alfredo sauce.

2 Cover and cook on low-heat setting for 4 to 5 hours or on high-heat setting for 2 to 2½ hours.

3 Cook pasta according to package directions. Drain. Stir pasta into mixture in slow cooker. To serve, spoon pasta mixture into shallow bowls. If desired, sprinkle with Parmesan cheese.

Nutrition Facts per serving: 407 cal., 11 g total fat (5 g sat. fat), 103 mg chol., 447 mg sodium, 39 g carbo., 2 g fiber, 36 g pro.
Daily Values: 77% vit. A, 10% vit. C, 9% calcium, 19% iron

Country-Style Smoked Sausage and Sauerkraut

Got a craving for sauerkraut? With potatoes and a little mustard, this dish will soon have you fed, sated, and happy.

Prep: 15 minutes Cook: Low 6 hours, High 3 hours Makes: 4 servings

10 to 12 tiny new potatoes, quartered (about 1 pound)
1 medium onion, cut into thin wedges
1 pound smoked turkey sausage, cut into 1-inch pieces
1 14- to 15-ounce can Bavarian-style sauerkraut (with caraway seeds),* undrained
⅓ cup water
1 tablespoon Dijon-style mustard

1 In a 3½- or 4-quart slow cooker place potatoes and onion wedges. Top with sausage and undrained sauerkraut.

2 In a small bowl whisk together water and mustard; pour over sauerkraut.

3 Cover and cook on low-heat setting for 6 to 8 hours or on high-heat setting for 3 to 4 hours.

***Note:** *If Bavarian-style sauerkraut is not available, substitute one 14½-ounce can sauerkraut plus 2 tablespoons packed brown sugar and ½ teaspoon caraway seeds.*

Nutrition Facts per serving: 317 cal., 10 g total fat (2 g sat. fat), 76 mg chol., 3,472 mg sodium, 37 g carbo., 2 g fiber, 21 g pro.
Daily Values: 36% vit. C, 3% calcium, 17% iron

BBQ Beans and Franks over Corn Bread

Dreaming of sunny days and picnic fare? This easy main dish can take you there.

Prep: 10 minutes Cook: Low 5 hours, High 2½ hours Makes: 6 servings

- 2 15-ounce cans pork and beans in tomato sauce, undrained
- 2 15- to 16-ounce cans black beans and/or pinto beans, rinsed and drained
- ⅔ cup bottled barbecue sauce
- 16 ounces cooked turkey franks, cut crosswise into fourths
- Purchased corn bread

1 In a 3½- or 4-quart slow cooker combine undrained pork and beans, drained black beans, barbecue sauce, and turkey franks.

2 Cover and cook on low-heat setting for 5 to 6 hours or on high-heat setting for 2½ to 3 hours.

3 To serve, cut corn bread into 6 pieces. Place a corn bread piece in each of 6 shallow bowls. Spoon beans and franks over the top.

Nutrition Facts per serving: 596 cal., 21 g total fat (6 g sat. fat), 112 mg chol., 2,541 mg sodium, 78 g carbo., 15 g fiber, 30 g pro. Daily Values: 13% vit. A, 4% vit. C, 36% calcium, 35% iron

3

Main Dishes Starring Beef, Pork, and Lamb

Pot Roast with Chipotle-Fruit Sauce

You can adjust the amount of chipotle peppers, depending on how much heat you like.

Prep: 20 minutes Cook: Low 10 hours, High 5 hours Makes: 6 to 8 servings

- 1 3-pound boneless beef chuck pot roast
- 2 teaspoons garlic-pepper seasoning
- 1 7-ounce package mixed dried fruit
- ½ cup water
- 1 tablespoon finely chopped chipotle peppers in adobo sauce
- 1 tablespoon cold water
- 2 teaspoons cornstarch

1 Sprinkle both sides of meat with garlic-pepper seasoning. If necessary, cut meat to fit into a 3½- or 4-quart slow cooker. Place meat in the cooker. Add fruit, the ½ cup water, and peppers.

2 Cover and cook on low-heat setting for 10 to 11 hours or on high-heat setting for 5 to 5½ hours. Transfer meat and fruit to a serving platter. Cover and keep warm.

3 Transfer cooking liquid to a bowl or glass measuring cup; skim off fat. In a medium saucepan combine the 1 tablespoon water and the cornstarch; add cooking liquid. Cook and stir until thickened and bubbly; cook and stir for 2 minutes more. Thinly slice meat. Spoon sauce over sliced meat and fruit.

Nutrition Facts per serving: 576 cal., 19 g total fat (7 g sat. fat), 229 mg chol., 502 mg sodium, 23 g carbo., 1 g fiber, 76 g pro.
Daily Values: 2% vit. C, 3% calcium, 53% iron

Cola Pot Roast

Different and delicious, this chuck roast with veggies and gravy gets its sweet kick from a can of cola. The meat is tender; the gravy is thick.

Prep: 15 minutes Cook: Low 7 hours, High 3½ hours Makes: 6 servings

- 1 2½- to 3-pound boneless beef chuck pot roast
- Nonstick cooking spray
- 2 16-ounce packages frozen loose-pack stew vegetables
- 1 12-ounce can cola
- 1 envelope (½ of a 2-ounce package) onion soup mix
- 2 tablespoons quick-cooking tapioca

1 Trim fat from meat. Lightly coat a large skillet with cooking spray; heat over medium heat. In hot skillet cook meat until brown on all sides.

2 Place meat in a 4½- or 5-quart slow cooker. Top with frozen vegetables. In a small bowl stir together cola, soup mix, and tapioca. Pour over meat and vegetables in cooker.

3 Cover and cook on low-heat setting for 7 to 8 hours or on high-heat setting for 3½ to 4 hours.

Nutrition Facts per serving: 278 cal., 5 g total fat (2 g sat. fat), 75 mg chol., 582 mg sodium, 28 g carbo., 2 g fiber, 29 g pro.
Daily Values: 148% vit. A, 3% vit. C, 1% calcium, 17% iron

Pot Roast with Mushroom Sauce

Take 15 minutes in the morning to brown the roast, cut up the potatoes, and layer the ingredients in your cooker. At the end of the day, gather the family for a complete dinner.

Prep: 15 minutes Cook: Low 10 hours, High 5 hours Makes: 5 servings

- 1 1½-pound boneless beef eye round roast or rump roast
- Nonstick cooking spray
- 4 medium potatoes, quartered
- 1 16-ounce package peeled baby carrots
- 1 10¾-ounce can condensed golden mushroom soup
- ½ teaspoon dried tarragon or basil, crushed

1 Trim fat from meat. Lightly coat a large skillet with cooking spray; heat over medium heat. In hot skillet cook meat until brown on all sides.

2 In a 3½- or 4-quart slow cooker place potatoes and carrots. Place meat on top of vegetables. In a bowl stir together soup and tarragon; pour over meat in cooker.

3 Cover and cook on low-heat setting for 10 to 12 hours or on high-heat setting for 5 to 6 hours. Transfer meat and vegetables to a serving platter. Stir sauce; spoon over meat and vegetables.

Nutrition Facts per serving: 391 cal., 13 g total fat (5 g sat. fat), 79 mg chol., 567 mg sodium, 33 g carbo., 5 g fiber, 33 g pro.
Daily Values: 237% vit. A, 38% vit. C, 4% calcium, 19% iron

Homestyle Beef and Vegetables

You can spoon this savory beef and veggie dish over noodles, but it's equally good on its own.

Prep: 20 minutes Cook: Low 8 hours, High 4 hours; plus 30 minutes on High Makes: 6 servings

Nonstick cooking spray
1 3- to 3½-pound boneless beef chuck roast
1 0.6-ounce envelope Italian dry salad dressing mix
3 tablespoons quick-cooking tapioca
1 14-ounce can beef broth seasoned with onion
1 16-ounce package frozen loose-pack Italian vegetables (zucchini, carrots, cauliflower, lima beans, Italian beans)

1 Lightly coat a 3½- or 4-quart slow cooker with cooking spray; set aside. Lightly coat a large skillet with cooking spray; heat over medium heat. Trim fat from meat. In hot skillet cook meat until brown on all sides.

2 Place meat in the prepared cooker. Sprinkle with salad dressing mix and tapioca. Pour broth over all.

3 Cover and cook on low-heat setting for 8 to 9 hours or on high-heat setting for 4 to 4½ hours. If using low-heat setting, turn to high-heat setting. Add frozen vegetables to cooker. Cover and cook about 30 minutes more or until tender.

Nutrition Facts per serving: 338 cal., 8 g total fat (3 g sat. fat), 134 mg chol., 787 mg sodium, 11 g carbo., 2 g fiber, 50 g pro.
Daily Values: 46% vit. A, 9% vit. C, 3% calcium, 31% iron

Cowboy Beef

Pot roast heads for the untamed West when slow cooked with chili beans, corn, tomatoes, and spicy chile peppers in adobo sauce. Corn bread is a quick and tasty side.

Prep: 10 minutes Cook: Low 10 hours, High 5 hours Makes: 6 servings

1 2- to 2½-pound boneless beef chuck pot roast
1 15-ounce can chili beans with chili gravy, undrained
1 11-ounce can whole kernel corn with sweet peppers, drained
1 10-ounce can chopped tomatoes and green chile peppers, undrained
1 to 2 teaspoons chipotle peppers in adobo sauce, finely chopped

1 Trim fat from meat. If necessary, cut roast to fit into a 3½- or 4-quart slow cooker. Place meat in the cooker. In a medium bowl combine undrained beans, corn, undrained tomatoes, and chipotle peppers. Pour bean mixture over meat in cooker.

2 Cover and cook on low-heat setting for 10 to 12 hours or on high-heat setting for 5 to 6 hours.

3 Remove meat from cooker and place on cutting board. Slice meat and arrange in a shallow serving bowl. Using a slotted spoon, spoon bean mixture over meat. Drizzle some of the cooking liquid over all.

Nutrition Facts per serving: 307 cal., 7 g total fat (2 g sat. fat), 89 mg chol., 655 mg sodium, 23 g carbo., 5 g fiber, 37 g pro.
Daily Values: 6% vit. A, 14% vit. C, 4% calcium, 28% iron

French Dips with Mushrooms

Slices of meaty portobello mushrooms add savory dimension to French dip sandwiches. Pour seasoned broth into dishes that are just large enough to dunk a portion of the sandwich.

Prep: 25 minutes Cook: Low 8 hours, High 4 hours Stand: 10 minutes Makes: 8 sandwiches

- 1 3- to 3½-pound beef bottom round or rump roast
- Nonstick cooking spray
- 4 portobello mushrooms (3 to 4 inches in diameter)
- 1 14-ounce can beef broth seasoned with onion
- 1 large red onion, cut into ½-inch slices
- 8 hoagie buns, split and toasted

1 Trim fat from meat. If necessary, cut meat to fit into a 3½- to 6-quart slow cooker. Lightly coat a large skillet with cooking spray; heat over medium heat. In hot skillet cook meat until brown on all sides. Place meat in the prepared cooker.

2 Clean mushrooms; remove and discard stems. Cut mushrooms into ¼-inch slices. Add to cooker. Pour broth over meat and mushrooms.

3 Cover and cook on low-heat setting for 8 to 9 hours or on high-heat setting for 4 to 4½ hours. Remove meat from cooker; cover and let stand for 10 minutes.

4 Meanwhile, using a slotted spoon, remove mushrooms and set aside. Thinly slice meat. Arrange meat, mushroom slices, and onion slices on toasted buns. Pour cooking juices into a measuring cup; skim off fat. Drizzle a little of the juices onto each sandwich and pour the remaining juices into individual dishes to serve with sandwiches for dipping.

Nutrition Facts per sandwich: 780 cal., 33 g total fat (11 g sat. fat), 106 mg chol., 955 mg sodium, 73 g carbo., 4 g fiber, 47 g pro.
Daily Values: 11% calcium, 42% iron

Beer Brisket

Pack some tang, pack some heat. Your tools are beer and chili sauce, which do great things to beef brisket and sliced onions. Fork slices of meat onto kaiser rolls for a hearty sandwich.

Prep: 15 minutes Cook: Low 10 hours, High 5 hours Makes: 9 to 12 servings

1 3- to 4-pound fresh beef brisket
2 large onions, sliced
1 12-ounce bottle or can beer
½ cup bottled chili sauce
2 teaspoons dried steak seasoning
9 to 12 kaiser rolls, split and toasted (optional)

1 Trim fat from meat. If necessary, cut meat to fit into a 3½- or 4-quart slow cooker. Place onions in cooker. Top with meat. In a medium bowl stir together beer, chili sauce, and steak seasoning. Pour over onions and meat in cooker.

2 Cover and cook on low-heat setting for 10 to 12 hours or on high-heat setting for 5 to 6 hours.

3 To serve, remove meat from cooking liquid. Thinly slice meat across the grain. Using a slotted spoon, remove the onions from the cooking liquid and place on top of the meat. Drizzle with some of the cooking liquid. If desired, serve sliced meat and onions on kaiser rolls.

Nutrition Facts per serving: 265 cal., 10 g total fat (4 g sat. fat), 94 mg chol., 378 mg sodium, 8 g carbo., 2 g fiber, 31 g pro.
Daily Values: 2% vit. A, 7% vit. C, 2% calcium, 17% iron

Asian Beef Short Ribs

Plum sauce, rice vinegar, and fresh grated ginger are your passports to exotic flavor. A side dish of steamed rice absorbs the extra sauce.

Prep: 25 minutes Cook: Low 6 hours, High 3 hours Makes: 6 servings

- 3 pounds boneless beef short ribs
- 1 7.6-ounce jar plum sauce
- ⅔ cup catsup
- 1 tablespoon rice vinegar
- 2 teaspoons grated fresh ginger

1 In a large nonstick skillet cook meat over medium-high heat until brown on both sides. Place meat in a 3½- or 4-quart slow cooker. In a medium bowl stir together plum sauce, catsup, vinegar, and ginger. Pour over meat.

2 Cover and cook on low-heat setting for 6 to 8 hours or on high-heat setting for 3 to 4 hours. Using a slotted spoon, transfer meat to a serving platter. Skim fat from cooking liquid; spoon some of the cooking liquid over meat.

Nutrition Facts per serving: 245 cal., 8 g total fat (3 g sat. fat), 53 mg chol., 538 mg sodium, 25 g carbo., 0 g fiber, 18 g pro.
Daily Values: 6% vit. A, 8% vit. C, 2% calcium, 15% iron

Beef Burgundy

The sophistication of Burgundy wine adds a deep woody taste that is mellowed with stew vegetables. Hot cooked noodles or mashed potatoes are a must.

Prep: 20 minutes Cook: Low 7 hours, High 3½ hours Makes: 6 servings

- 2 pounds beef stew meat
- Nonstick cooking spray
- 1 16-ounce package frozen loose-pack stew vegetables
- 1 10¾-ounce can condensed golden mushroom soup
- ⅔ cup Burgundy wine
- ⅓ cup water
- 1 tablespoon quick-cooking tapioca

1 If necessary, cut up large pieces of meat. Lightly coat a large skillet with cooking spray; heat over medium heat. In hot skillet cook meat, half at a time, until brown. Drain off fat. Set aside.

2 Place frozen vegetables in a 3½- or 4-quart slow cooker. Top with meat. In a medium bowl stir together soup, wine, water, and tapioca. Pour over meat and vegetables in cooker.

3 Cover and cook on low-heat setting for 7 to 9 hours or on high-heat setting for 3½ to 4½ hours.

Nutrition Facts per serving: 291 cal., 8 g total fat (3 g sat. fat), 91 mg chol., 535 mg sodium, 14 g carbo., 1 g fiber, 34 g pro.
Daily Values: 80% vit. A, 2% vit. C, 1% calcium, 23% iron

Oriental Beef and Noodles

Sesame-ginger stir-fry sauce infuses just the right amount of nutty zing. Add crushed red pepper if you opt for extra heat.

Prep: 10 minutes Cook: Low 9 hours, High 4½ hours Stand: 10 minutes Makes: 4 to 6 servings

- 1 16-ounce package frozen loose-pack broccoli stir-fry vegetables (broccoli, carrot, onion, red sweet pepper, celery, water chestnuts, mushrooms)
- 2 pounds beef stew meat
- 1 12-ounce bottle sesame-ginger stir-fry sauce
- ½ cup water
- ¼ teaspoon crushed red pepper (optional)
- 1 3-ounce package ramen noodles, broken

1 Place frozen vegetables in a 3½- or 4-quart slow cooker. Top with meat. In a medium bowl combine stir-fry sauce, water, and, if desired, crushed red pepper. Pour over meat and vegetables in cooker.

2 Cover and cook on low-heat setting for 9 to 10 hours or on high-heat setting for 4½ to 5 hours. Discard spice packet from ramen noodles. Stir noodles into meat mixture in slow cooker. Cover and let stand 10 minutes. Stir before serving.

Nutrition Facts per serving: 494 cal., 11 g total fat (2 g sat. fat), 135 mg chol., 1,889 mg sodium, 37 g carbo., 2 g fiber, 53 g pro.
Daily Values: 30% vit. A, 43% vit. C, 2% calcium, 32% iron

Easy Beef Stroganoff

When the weather forecast is wicked, hole up at home with board games, cozy blankets, and this dish in the cooker.

Prep: 15 minutes Cook: Low 8 hours, High 4 hours Makes: 6 servings

- 2 pounds boneless beef round, cut into 1-inch cubes
- 2 10¾-ounce cans condensed golden mushroom soup
- 1 medium onion, sliced
- 1 8-ounce container dairy sour cream chive dip
- 3 cups hot cooked noodles

1 In a 3½- or 4-quart slow cooker stir together the meat, soup, and onion.

2 Cover and cook on low-heat setting for 8 to 10 hours or on high-heat setting for 4 to 5 hours. Stir in dip. Serve over hot cooked noodles.

Nutrition Facts per serving: 450 cal., 16 g total fat (7 g sat. fat), 131 mg chol., 1,155 mg sodium, 33 g carbo., 2 g fiber, 42 g pro.
Daily Values: 19% vit. A, 2% vit. C, 6% calcium, 27% iron

Steak with Mushrooms

If you're a meat and potatoes type and you can't imagine having one without the other, cook a package of frozen mashed potatoes to serve with this saucy round steak.

Prep: 10 minutes Cook: Low 8 hours, High 4 hours Makes: 4 servings

- 1 pound boneless beef round steak, cut 1 inch thick
- 2 medium onions, sliced
- 2 4½-ounce jars whole mushrooms, drained
- 1 12-ounce jar beef gravy
- ¼ cup dry red wine or apple juice

1 Trim fat from meat. Cut meat into 4 serving-size pieces. Place onion slices in a 3½- or 4-quart slow cooker. Arrange mushrooms over onions; add meat. In a bowl stir together gravy and wine. Pour over meat.

2 Cover and cook on low-heat setting for 8 to 10 hours or on high-heat setting for 4 to 5 hours.

Nutrition Facts per serving: 220 cal., 4 g total fat (2 g sat. fat), 51 mg chol., 814 mg sodium, 11 g carbo., 3 g fiber, 31 g pro.
Daily Values: 3% vit. A, 3% calcium, 20% iron

Slow-Cooked Beef Fajitas

Set the table with tortillas, a platter of seasoned shredded meat, and a bowl of sour cream. Then let your dinner companions roll their own meals.

Prep: 15 minutes Cook: Low 8 hours, High 4 hours Makes: 8 servings

- 1½ pounds beef flank steak
- 1 16-ounce package frozen loose-pack pepper stir-fry vegetables (yellow, green, and red sweet peppers and onion)
- 1 16-ounce jar green salsa (about 1¾ cups)
- 8 9- to 10-inch flour tortillas, warmed*
- ½ cup dairy sour cream

1 Trim fat from meat. If necessary, cut meat into portions to fit into a 3½- or 4-quart slow cooker.

2 Place stir-fry vegetables in the cooker. Top with meat. Pour salsa over all.

3 Cover and cook on low-heat setting for 8 to 10 hours or on high-heat setting for 4 to 5 hours. Remove meat from cooker; slice across the grain. Strain peppers, reserving ⅓ cup of the liquid. Stir meat and ⅓ cup of the reserved juices into vegetables. Serve in tortillas and top with sour cream.

***Note:** *To warm tortillas, stack tortillas and wrap tightly in foil. Heat in a 350°F oven about 10 minutes or until heated through.*

Nutrition Facts per serving: 325 cal., 12 g total fat (5 g sat. fat), 39 mg chol., 463 mg sodium, 30 g carbo., 3 g fiber, 23 g pro.
Daily Values: 2% vit. A, 8% vit. C, 10% calcium, 16% iron

Southwestern Steak Roll-Ups

Simmering flank steak, peppers, onions, and tomatoes spiked with chili powder results in a mixture that tastes great wrapped in a warm tortilla.

Prep: 15 minutes Cook: Low 7 hours, High 3½ hours Makes: 4 servings

- 1 16-ounce package frozen loose-pack pepper stir-fry vegetables (yellow, green, and red sweet peppers and onion)
- 1 pound beef flank steak
- 1 14½-ounce can Mexican-style stewed tomatoes, undrained
- 1 small jalapeño pepper, seeded and finely chopped* (optional)
- 2 teaspoons chili powder
- 4 9- to 10-inch flour tortillas, warmed**

1 Place frozen vegetables in a 3½- or 4-quart slow cooker. Trim fat from meat. If necessary, cut meat to fit in cooker. Place meat on top of vegetables in cooker. In a medium bowl stir together undrained tomatoes; if desired, jalapeño pepper; and chili powder. Pour over meat in cooker.

2 Cover and cook on low-heat setting for 7 to 8 hours or on high-heat setting for 3½ to 4 hours. Remove meat from cooker; slice against the grain. Using a slotted spoon, remove vegetables from cooker. Divide meat and vegetables among warm tortillas; roll up.

***Note:** *Because hot chile peppers, such as jalapeños, contain volatile oils that can burn your skin and eyes, avoid direct contact with chiles as much as possible. When working with chile peppers, wear plastic or rubber gloves. If your bare hands do touch the chile peppers, wash your hands well with soap and water.*

****Note:** *To warm tortillas, stack tortillas and wrap tightly in foil. Heat in a 350°F oven about 10 minutes or until heated through.*

Nutrition Facts per serving: 389 cal., 12 g total fat (5 g sat. fat), 46 mg chol., 647 mg sodium, 36 g carbo., 4 g fiber, 32 g pro.
Daily Values: 29% vit. A, 54% vit. C, 10% calcium, 24% iron

Thai Beef

Those who love pad thai's signature peanut sauce will adore this easy-to-prepare dish of tender flank steak and carrots. Fluffy hot cooked rice is the perfect complement.

Prep: 15 minutes Cook: Low 8 hours, High 4 hours Makes: 6 servings

- 1 1½- to 2-pound beef flank steak
- 1 16-ounce package peeled baby carrots
- 1 11½-ounce bottle Thai peanut sauce
- 1 cup unsweetened coconut milk
- ¼ cup chopped dry roasted peanuts

1 Trim fat from steak. Cut meat into thin bite-size strips. In a 3½- or 4-quart slow cooker place meat strips and carrots. Pour peanut sauce over all.

2 Cover and cook on low-heat setting for 8 to 10 hours or on high-heat setting for 4 to 5 hours. Stir in coconut milk. Sprinkle each serving with peanuts.

Nutrition Facts per serving: 449 cal., 25 g total fat (12 g sat. fat), 46 mg chol., 814 mg sodium, 23 g carbo., 6 g fiber, 31 g pro.
Daily Values: 384% vit. A, 11% vit. C, 4% calcium, 18% iron

Corned Beef and Cabbage

Plan this Irish classic for St. Paddy's Day. Enjoy it with a mug of cold beer.

Prep: 15 minutes Cook: Low 10 hours, High 5 hours Makes: 6 servings

- 1 3- to 4-pound corned beef brisket with spice packet
- ½ small head cabbage, cut into 3 wedges
- 4 medium carrots, peeled and cut into 2-inch pieces
- 1 medium onion, quartered
- 2 medium yellow potatoes, cut into 2-inch pieces
- ½ cup water

1 Trim fat from meat. If necessary, cut meat to fit into a 5- to 6-quart slow cooker. Sprinkle spices from packet evenly over meat; rub in with your fingers. Place cabbage, carrots, onion, and potatoes in the cooker. Pour water over vegetables. Top with meat.

2 Cover and cook on low-heat setting for 10 to 12 hours or on high-heat setting for 5 to 6 hours. Transfer meat to a cutting board; thinly slice meat against the grain. Remove vegetables with a slotted spoon. Serve meat and vegetables on a platter.

Nutrition Facts per serving: 457 cal., 27 g total fat (7 g sat. fat), 115 mg chol., 1,543 mg sodium, 16 g carbo., 3 g fiber, 35 g pro.
Daily Values: 207% vit. A, 123% vit. C, 5% calcium, 28% iron

Reubens from a Crock

Here's a decadent party-pleaser that's easy on the hosts. Those who love Reubens will applaud you.

Prep: 15 minutes Cook: Low 4 hours, High 2 hours Makes: 8 sandwiches

- 1 2- to 3-pound corned beef brisket with spice packet
- 1 16-ounce jar sauerkraut, drained
- ½ cup bottled Thousand Island salad dressing
- 16 slices rye swirl bread, toasted
- 8 ounces sliced Swiss cheese
- Bottled Thousand Island salad dressing (optional)

1 Trim fat from meat. If necessary, cut meat to fit into a 3½- or 4-quart slow cooker. Place meat in cooker. Sprinkle spices from packet evenly over meat. Spread sauerkraut over meat. Drizzle the ½ cup salad dressing over all.

2 Cover and cook on low-heat setting for 4 to 6 hours or on high-heat setting for 2 to 3 hours. Remove meat from cooker and place on cutting board. Thinly slice meat against the grain. Return sliced meat to the cooker and stir to combine with the cooking liquid.

3 Using a slotted spoon, spoon corned beef mixture onto 8 slices of the toasted bread. Top with cheese; if desired, additional salad dressing; and remaining bread.

Nutrition Facts per sandwich: 564 cal., 34 g total fat (10 g sat. fat), 89 mg chol., 2,101 mg sodium, 35 g carbo., 4 g fiber, 29 g pro.
Daily Values: 7% vit. A, 52% vit. C, 28% calcium, 22% iron

Irish Grinders

These tasty corned beef and cabbage sandwiches are guaranteed to bring out the Irish in you. Add them to your St. Patrick's Day menu.

Prep: 20 minutes Cook: Low 8 hours, High 4 hours Makes: 8 servings

- 1 2- to 3-pound corned beef brisket with spice packet
- 1 cup water
- ⅓ cup Dijon-style mustard
- 2 teaspoons prepared horseradish
- 4 cups coarsely shredded cabbage
- 8 kaiser rolls, split and toasted
- Dijon-style mustard (optional)

1 Trim fat from meat. Sprinkle spices from packet evenly over meat; rub in with your fingers. If necessary, cut meat to fit into a 3½- or 4-quart slow cooker. Place meat in the cooker. In a small bowl combine water, the ⅓ cup mustard, and horseradish. Pour mustard mixture over meat. Top with cabbage.

2 Cover and cook on low-heat setting for 8 to 10 hours or on high-heat setting for 4 to 5 hours.

3 Transfer meat to a cutting board. Thinly slice meat across the grain. Arrange meat slices on roll bottoms. Using a slotted spoon, place some of the cooked cabbage on meat. If desired, spread additional mustard on roll tops. Add roll tops.

Nutrition Facts per serving: 391 cal., 17 g total fat (4 g sat. fat), 58 mg chol., 482 mg sodium, 34 g carbo., 2 g fiber, 24 g pro.
Daily Values: 1% vit. A, 57% vit. C, 10% calcium, 24% iron

Beefy Mexican Potatoes

Cheesy bean-and-beef chili floods baked potatoes for a rib-sticking meal. The chili topper also makes a hearty dip for corn chips or the meaty addition to a taco salad.

Prep: 15 minutes Cook: Low 3 hours Microwave: 15 minutes Makes: 6 servings

Nonstick cooking spray
1 20-ounce package refrigerated seasoned cooked ground beef for tacos
2 15- to 16-ounce cans red kidney and/or black beans, rinsed and drained
1 10-ounce can enchilada sauce
2 cups shredded American cheese (8 ounces)
6 baking potatoes

1 Coat a 3½- or 4-quart slow cooker with cooking spray. In the prepared cooker combine meat, beans, enchilada sauce, and 1½ cups of the cheese.

2 Cover and cook on low-heat setting for 3 to 4 hours.

3 Meanwhile, prick potatoes all over with a fork. Arrange potatoes in spoke-fashion on a microwave-safe plate. Microwave, uncovered, on 100 percent power (high) for 15 to 18 minutes or until tender, rearranging potatoes every 5 minutes. (Or bake pricked potatoes in a 450°F oven for 40 to 60 minutes.) Carefully cut a cross in the top of each potato. Push in longer sides to open potato. Stir beef mixture in cooker. Spoon beef mixture over baked potatoes. Top with remaining cheese.

Nutrition Facts per serving: 553 cal., 22 g total fat (11 g sat. fat), 61 mg chol., 1,560 mg sodium, 64 g carbo., 11 g fiber, 32 g pro.
Daily Values: 17% vit. A, 22% vit. C, 32% calcium, 25% iron

Italian Meat Loaf

Shaped to avoid touching the slow cooker edges, this simple meat loaf lifts out easily so you can place it on a platter and serve it at the table.

Prep: 15 minutes Cook: Low 5 hours, High 2½ hours Stand: 10 minutes Makes: 6 to 8 servings

- 1 egg, beaten
- 1 8-ounce can pizza sauce
- ½ cup seasoned fine dry bread crumbs
- 2 pounds lean ground beef
- ¼ cup shredded Monterey Jack cheese, mozzarella cheese, or Parmesan cheese (1 ounce)

1 In a large bowl combine egg, ½ cup of the pizza sauce, and the bread crumbs. Add ground meat and mix well.

2 On waxed paper, shape meat mixture into a 6-inch round loaf. Crisscross three 18×2-inch foil strips. Place meat loaf in center of strips. Bringing up foil strips, lift and transfer meat to a 3½- or 4-quart slow cooker using the foil strips. Press meat away from sides of cooker to avoid burning.

3 Cover and cook on low-heat setting for 5 to 6 hours or on high-heat setting for 2½ to 3 hours. Using foil strips, carefully lift meat loaf from the cooker and transfer to a serving plate. Spoon remaining pizza sauce over meat; sprinkle with cheese. Let stand 10 minutes before slicing.

Nutrition Facts per serving: 327 cal., 17 g total fat (7 g sat. fat), 135 mg chol., 541 mg sodium, 11 g carbo., 1 g fiber, 31 g pro.
Daily Values: 2% vit. A, 6% vit. C, 6% calcium, 17% iron

Mexican Stuffed Sweet Peppers

The shells of colorful sweet peppers provide a crisp, cool complement to their contents: warm ground meat, spicy cheese, and zesty salsa.

Prep: 25 minutes Cook: Low 6 hours, High 3 hours Makes: 4 servings

- 4 medium green, red, and/or yellow sweet peppers
- 1 pound lean ground beef or ground pork
- 1 cup quick-cooking white rice
- 6 ounces Monterey Jack cheese with jalapeño peppers or Monterey Jack cheese, shredded (1½ cups)
- 1 16-ounce jar bottled black bean salsa or chunky salsa
- 1 cup water

1 Remove tops of sweet peppers; scoop out membranes and seeds. Set aside. For filling, in a large skillet cook ground meat until brown. Drain off fat. Stir in rice, 1 cup of the cheese, and the salsa. Spoon filling into peppers; mound tops as needed.

2 Place the water into a 4½- or 5-quart slow cooker. Arrange stuffed peppers, filling side up, in the cooker.

3 Cover and cook on low-heat setting for 6 to 7 hours or on high-heat setting for 3 to 3½ hours. Transfer peppers to a serving platter. Top with remaining cheese.

Nutrition Facts per serving: 513 cal., 24 g total fat (12 g sat. fat), 109 mg chol., 1,060 mg sodium, 38 g carbo., 2 g fiber, 37 g pro. Daily Values: 29% vit. A, 171% vit. C, 33% calcium, 21% iron

Easy Goulash

Hailing from Hungary, goulash features the zest of tomatoes, garlic, and oregano. Keep it traditional and serve it with buttered noodles.

Prep: 20 minutes Cook: Low 6 hours, High 3 hours Stand: 5 minutes Makes: 4 servings

- 1 pound lean ground beef
- ½ of a 28-ounce package frozen loose-pack diced hash brown potatoes with onion and peppers (about 3½ cups)
- 1 15-ounce can tomato sauce
- 1 14½-ounce can diced tomatoes with basil, garlic, and oregano, undrained
- ½ cup shredded cheddar cheese (2 ounces)

1 In a large skillet cook ground meat over medium heat until brown. Drain off fat.

2 In a 3½- or 4-quart slow cooker combine meat, frozen potatoes, tomato sauce, and undrained tomatoes.

3 Cover and cook on low-heat setting for 6 to 8 hours or on high-heat setting for 3 to 4 hours. Remove liner from cooker or turn off cooker. Sprinkle meat mixture with cheese. Let stand 5 minutes or until cheese melts.

Nutrition Facts per serving: 535 cal., 33 g total fat (14 g sat. fat), 109 mg chol., 1,371 mg sodium, 34 g carbo., 4 g fiber, 27 g pro.
Daily Values: 39% vit. A, 54% vit. C, 20% calcium, 30% iron

Beefy Shepherd's Pie

This dish is for those who are nostalgic for homey foods. The sprinkling of shredded cheddar cheese before serving is optional.

Prep: 20 minutes Cook: Low 6 hours, High 3 hours Makes: 8 servings

- 2 pounds lean ground beef
- 1 cup chopped onion (1 large)
- 1 16-ounce package frozen mixed vegetables
- 2 10¾-ounce cans condensed tomato soup
- 8 servings refrigerated or frozen mashed potatoes

1 In a large skillet cook ground meat and onion until meat is brown and onion is tender; drain off fat.

2 In a 3½- or 4-quart slow cooker combine meat mixture, frozen mixed vegetables, and soup.

3 Cover and cook on low-heat setting for 6 to 8 hours or on high-heat setting for 3 to 4 hours.

4 Meanwhile, prepare mashed potatoes according to package directions. Serve meat mixture with potatoes.

Nutrition Facts per serving: 575 cal., 27 g total fat (13 g sat. fat), 106 mg chol., 836 mg sodium, 51 g carbo., 7 g fiber, 32 g pro.
Daily Values: 72% vit. A, 56% vit. C, 9% calcium, 27% iron

Tostadas

Turn to this soft, chunky Mexican classic when you want the convenience of leaving a meal unattended but need it prepared in a short time.

Prep: 15 minutes Cook: Low 3 hours, High 1½ hours Makes: 10 servings

- 2 pounds lean ground beef
- 2 1¼-ounce envelopes taco seasoning mix
- 1 16-ounce can refried beans
- 1 10¾-ounce can condensed fiesta nacho cheese soup
- 1 4.8-ounce package tostada shells (10)
- Shredded lettuce, chopped tomatoes, dairy sour cream, and/or bottled salsa (optional)

1 In a large skillet cook ground meat until brown; drain off fat. Add taco seasoning mix to meat and continue according to package directions.

2 Transfer seasoned meat mixture to a 3½- or 4-quart slow cooker. Stir in refried beans and soup.

3 Cover and cook on low-heat setting for 3 to 4 hours or on high-heat setting for 1½ to 2 hours. Serve on tostada shells. If desired, top with lettuce, tomatoes, sour cream, and/or salsa.

Nutrition Facts per serving: 347 cal., 20 g total fat (6 g sat. fat), 65 mg chol., 1,198 mg sodium, 21 g carbo., 4 g fiber, 24 g pro.
Daily Values: 6% vit. A, 5% vit. C, 6% calcium, 15% iron

Easy Cheesy Sloppy Joes

This is a kid-favorite that adults like too. Sweet pickle slices taste great on top of the meat.

Prep: 20 minutes Cook: Low 4½ hours, High 2 hours Makes: 16 servings

- 2½ pounds lean ground beef
- 1 cup chopped onion (1 large)
- 2 10¾-ounce cans condensed fiesta nacho cheese soup
- ¾ cup catsup
- 16 hamburger buns, split and toasted

1 In a 12-inch skillet cook ground meat and onion over medium heat until meat is brown and onion is tender. Drain off fat.

2 In a 3½- or 4-quart slow cooker combine meat mixture, soup, and catsup.

3 Cover and cook on low-heat setting for 4½ to 5 hours or on high-heat setting for 2 to 2½ hours. Serve meat mixture in toasted buns.

Nutrition Facts per serving: 389 cal., 22 g total fat (9 g sat. fat), 63 mg chol., 680 mg sodium, 29 g carbo., 2 g fiber, 17 g pro.
Daily Values: 10% vit. A, 5% vit. C, 10% calcium, 16% iron

Veal Osso Buco

The optional gremolata—a seasoning blend of snipped fresh parsley, lemon peel, and garlic—gives this tender veal dish a spring-fresh quality (see the recipe below).

Prep: 20 minutes Cook: Low 8 hours, High 4 hours Makes: 4 to 6 servings

2½ to 3 pounds veal shank cross-cuts (4 to 6)
Salt and black pepper (optional)
¼ cup all-purpose flour
2 tablespoons cooking oil
2 14½-ounce cans diced tomatoes with basil, garlic, and oregano, undrained
½ cup dry red wine
Gremolata (optional)
Hot cooked rice (optional)

1 If desired, season meat with salt and pepper. Place flour in a shallow dish. Dip meat in flour to coat. In a large skillet cook meat, half at a time, in hot oil over medium-high heat, turning to brown evenly. Drain off fat.

2 Place meat in a 3½- or 4-quart slow cooker. Pour undrained tomatoes and red wine over meat.

3 Cover and cook on low-heat setting for 8 to 9 hours or on high-heat setting for 4 to 4½ hours. Using a slotted spoon, transfer meat and tomatoes to a serving dish. If desired, sprinkle with Gremolata and serve with hot cooked rice.

Nutrition Facts per serving: 397 cal., 9 g total fat (2 g sat. fat), 163 mg chol., 1,249 mg sodium, 25 g carbo., 2 g fiber, 46 g pro.
Daily Values: 24% vit. A, 24% vit. C, 18% calcium, 29% iron

Gremolata: *In a small bowl stir together ½ cup snipped fresh parsley, 2 teaspoons finely shredded lemon peel, and 1 teaspoon minced garlic.*

Pork Roast with Apricot Glaze

It's enough to make any mouth water: These succulent pork roast slices are dripping in a spicy apricot sauce.

Prep: 15 minutes Cook: Low 10 hours, High 5 hours Makes: 6 to 8 servings

1 3- to 3½-pound boneless pork shoulder roast
1 18-ounce jar apricot preserves
1 cup chopped onion (1 large)
¼ cup chicken broth
2 tablespoons Dijon-style mustard

1 Trim fat from meat. If necessary, cut meat to fit into a 3½- to 6-quart slow cooker. Place meat in cooker. In a small bowl combine preserves, onion, broth, and mustard; pour over meat.

2 Cover and cook on low-heat setting for 10 to 12 hours or on high-heat setting for 5 to 6 hours. Transfer meat to a serving plate. Skim fat from glaze. Spoon some of the glaze over the meat; discard any remaining glaze.

Nutrition Facts per serving: 456 cal., 10 g total fat (3 g sat. fat), 93 mg chol., 184 mg sodium, 61 g carbo., 2 g fiber, 29 g pro.
Daily Values: 17% vit. C, 5% calcium, 13% iron

Cranberry Pork Roast

Chili sauce spikes the tart cranberry glaze in this thick, tender, and saucy dish. Prepare to dish out seconds.

Prep: 10 minutes Cook: Low 8 hours, High 4 hours; plus 20 minutes on cooktop Makes: 6 servings

- Nonstick cooking spray
- 1 2½- to 3-pound pork shoulder roast
- 1 16-ounce package frozen stew vegetables
- 1 16-ounce can whole cranberry sauce
- ½ cup bottled chili sauce

1 Lightly coat a large skillet with cooking spray; heat over medium heat. In hot skillet cook meat until brown on all sides. Drain off fat.

2 Place meat in a 3½- or 4-quart slow cooker. Top with frozen vegetables. In a small bowl stir together cranberry sauce and chili sauce. Pour over meat and vegetables in cooker.

3 Cover and cook on low-heat setting for 8 to 9 hours or on high-heat setting for 4 to 4½ hours. Transfer meat and vegetables to a serving platter; keep warm.

4 Strain cooking juices and skim off fat. In a medium saucepan bring cooking juices to boiling. Reduce heat. Simmer, uncovered, for 20 minutes or until thickened and the volume is reduced by half. Pass with meat and vegetables.

Nutrition Facts per serving: 494 cal., 16 g total fat (5 g sat. fat), 140 mg chol., 833 mg sodium, 44 g carbo., 2 g fiber, 41 g pro.
Daily Values: 88% vit. A, 7% vit. C, 5% calcium, 14% iron

Ranch Pork Roast

This is no ordinary roast with potatoes. Made with a tangy sauce of cream cheese seasoned with ranch dressing, this one-dish meal stands in a category all its own.

Prep: 15 minutes Cook: Low 9 hours, High 4½ hours Makes: 6 servings

- 1 2½- to 3-pound boneless pork shoulder roast
- Nonstick cooking spray
- 1 pound new red-skinned potatoes, halved
- 1 10¾-ounce can condensed cream of chicken soup
- 1 8-ounce package cream cheese, cubed and softened
- 1 0.4-ounce envelope ranch dry salad dressing mix

1 Trim fat from meat. Lightly coat a large skillet with cooking spray; heat over medium heat. In a hot skillet cook meat until brown on all sides. Remove from heat.

2 Place potatoes in a 3½- or 4-quart slow cooker. Place meat over potatoes. In a medium bowl whisk together soup, cream cheese, and salad dressing mix. Spoon over meat and potatoes in cooker.

3 Cover and cook on low-heat setting for 9 to 10 hours or on high-heat setting for 4½ to 5 hours.

Nutrition Facts per serving: 521 cal., 31 g total fat (15 g sat. fat), 173 mg chol., 757 mg sodium, 16 g carbo., 1 g fiber, 42 g pro. Daily Values: 15% vit. A, 17% vit. C, 9% calcium, 21% iron

Apricot Pulled Pork

Pile tender shredded pork onto crusty kaiser buns or wrap it in a tortilla, if you like, but don't pass on the dried apricots (they're key to the full flavor).

Prep: 20 minutes Cook: Low 8 hours, High 4 hours Makes: 6 to 8 servings

Nonstick cooking spray
1 3- to 3½-pound boneless pork shoulder roast
1 10-ounce jar apricot spreadable fruit
1 cup bottled hot-style barbecue sauce
½ cup chopped sweet onion (1 medium)
½ cup snipped dried apricots

1 Lightly coat a 3½- or 4-quart slow cooker with cooking spray. Trim fat from meat. If necessary, cut meat to fit into cooker. Place meat in prepared cooker. In a medium bowl combine spreadable fruit, barbecue sauce, onion, and dried apricots. Pour over meat in cooker.

2 Cover and cook on low-heat setting for 8 to 10 hours or on high-heat setting for 4 to 5 hours.

3 Transfer meat to a cutting board. Using 2 forks, gently shred the meat. In a large bowl combine shredded meat and some of the sauce from the cooker. Pass remaining sauce.

Nutrition Facts per serving: 535 cal., 19 g total fat (7 g sat. fat), 166 mg chol., 513 mg sodium, 42 g carbo., 2 g fiber, 49 g pro.
Daily Values: 15% vit. A, 9% vit. C, 7% calcium, 21% iron

Sauerkraut and Pork Shoulder Roast

The first night, serve this German-style pork with mashed potatoes, noodles, or boiled new potatoes. Another night, make open-face sandwiches with the leftovers (see the recipe below).

Prep: 15 minutes Cook: Low 8 hours, High 4 hours Makes: 8 servings

- 1 14- to 15-ounce can Bavarian-style sauerkraut (with caraway seeds), rinsed and drained
- 1 2½-pound boneless pork shoulder roast or pork sirloin roast
- Salt and black pepper
- 2 tablespoons creamy Dijon-style mustard blend
- 1 cup beer or nonalcoholic beer

1 Place sauerkraut in a 3½- or 4-quart slow cooker. Trim fat from meat. If necessary, cut meat to fit into the slow cooker. Lightly sprinkle meat with salt and pepper. Spread mustard over meat. Place meat on top of sauerkraut. Add the beer.

2 Cover and cook on low-heat setting for 8 to 10 hours or on high-heat setting for 4 to 5 hours. Transfer meat to a cutting board; cool slightly. Slice meat; discard fat. Serve sauerkraut with meat.

Nutrition Facts per serving: 230 cal., 10 g total fat (3 g sat. fat), 92 mg chol., 546 mg sodium, 4 g carbo., 1 g fiber, 29 g pro.
Daily Values: 15% vit. C, 3% calcium, 14% iron

Open-Face Pork Sandwiches: *Toast rye bread slices; spread with creamy Dijon-style mustard blend. Arrange bread slices on a baking sheet. Using 2 forks, gently shred meat. Top each bread slice with drained sauerkraut, shredded pork, and shredded Swiss cheese. Place baking sheet under broiler 3 to 4 inches from the heat. Broil for 2 to 3 minutes or until cheese melts.*

Hot Pepper Pork Sandwiches

You can adjust the heat level by varying the number of jalapeños you use. For even more heat, don't seed the peppers.

Prep: 20 minutes Cook: Low 11 hours, High 5½ hours Makes: 8 servings

1 2½- to 3-pound boneless pork shoulder roast
2 teaspoons fajita seasoning
2 10-ounce cans enchilada sauce
1 or 2 jalapeño peppers, seeded (if desired) and finely chopped,* or 1 large green or red sweet pepper, seeded and cut into bite-size strips
8 kaiser rolls, split and toasted

1 Trim fat from meat. If necessary, cut meat to fit into a 3½- to 5-quart slow cooker. Place meat in cooker. Sprinkle meat with the fajita seasoning. Add enchilada sauce and peppers.

2 Cover and cook on low-heat setting for 11 to 12 hours or on high-heat setting for 5½ to 6 hours. Transfer meat to a cutting board. Using 2 forks, gently shred the meat. Stir shredded meat into sauce mixture in slow cooker. Using a slotted spoon, spoon shredded meat mixture into toasted buns.

***Note:** *Because hot chile peppers, such as jalapeños, contain volatile oils that can burn your skin and eyes, avoid direct contact with chiles as much as possible. When working with chile peppers, wear plastic or rubber gloves. If your bare hands do touch the chile peppers, wash your hands well with soap and water.*

Nutrition Facts per serving: 316 cal., 9 g total fat (2 g sat. fat), 58 mg chol., 891 mg sodium, 34 g carbo., 2 g fiber, 23 g pro.
Daily Values: 4% vit. A, 6% vit. C, 8% calcium, 19% iron

Cajun Pork

The deep South is known for hot weather and even hotter food. This pork stew bears only mild Cajun seasoning—a good introduction for folks new to the flavor.

Prep: 20 minutes Cook: Low 6 hours, High 3 hours; plus 30 minutes on High
Makes: 6 to 8 servings

Nonstick cooking spray
2½ to 3 pounds boneless pork shoulder, trimmed of fat and cut into 1-inch cubes
2 medium yellow sweet peppers, cut into 1-inch pieces
1 tablespoon Cajun seasoning
1 14½-ounce can diced tomatoes with green pepper and onion, undrained
1 16-ounce package frozen cut okra
Bottled hot pepper sauce (optional)

1 Lightly coat a large skillet with cooking spray; heat over medium heat. In hot skillet cook meat, half at a time, until brown. Drain off fat.

2 In a 3½- or 4-quart slow cooker place meat and sweet peppers. Sprinkle with Cajun seasoning. Top with undrained tomatoes.

3 Cover and cook on low-heat setting for 6 to 7 hours or on high-heat setting for 3 to 3½ hours.

4 If using low-heat setting, turn to high-heat setting. Stir in frozen okra. Cover and cook 30 minutes more. If desired, pass hot pepper sauce.

Nutrition Facts per serving: 233 cal., 8 g total fat (3 g sat. fat), 77 mg chol., 444 mg sodium, 15 g carbo., 4 g fiber, 25 g pro.
Daily Values: 10% vit. A, 187% vit. C, 10% calcium, 14% iron

Slow-Cooked Asian-Style Pork

With its long cooking time, this dish is ideal for those who head out to work in the morning. Pieces of pork cook with stir-fry vegetables in a sweet-and-sour sauce.

Prep: 20 minutes Cook: Low 7 hours, High 3½ hours; plus 30 minutes on High
Makes: 6 to 8 servings

- Nonstick cooking spray
- 3 pounds boneless pork shoulder, cut into 1-inch pieces
- 2 tablespoons quick-cooking tapioca
- 1 10-ounce jar sweet-and-sour sauce
- 1 16-ounce package frozen loose-pack broccoli stir-fry vegetables (broccoli, carrots, onions, red sweet peppers, celery, water chestnuts, mushrooms)
- 3 cups hot cooked rice or rice noodles

1 Lightly coat a large skillet with cooking spray; heat over medium heat. In hot skillet cook meat, half at a time, until brown. Drain off fat.

2 Place meat in a 3½- or 4-quart slow cooker. Sprinkle with tapioca; pour sweet-and-sour sauce over meat in cooker.

3 Cover and cook on low-heat setting for 7 to 8 hours or on high-heat setting for 3½ to 4 hours. If using low-heat setting, turn to high-heat setting. Stir in frozen vegetables. Cover and cook for 30 to 60 minutes more or until vegetables are tender. Serve over hot cooked rice.

Nutrition Facts per serving: 484 cal., 19 g total fat (6 g sat. fat), 153 mg chol., 342 mg sodium, 40 g carbo., 2 g fiber, 48 g pro.
Daily Values: 20% vit. A, 30% vit. C, 6% calcium, 21% iron

Honey-Mustard Barbecue Pork Ribs

The simple pleasure of eating ribs that fall right off the bone starts with a simple blend of seasonings, barbecue sauce, and a jar of honey mustard.

Prep: 15 minutes Cook: Low 8 hours, High 4 hours Makes: 6 to 8 servings

3½ pounds boneless pork country-style ribs
1 cup bottled barbecue sauce
1 8-ounce jar honey mustard
2 teaspoons zesty herb grill seasoning blend

1 Place ribs in a 3½- or 4-quart slow cooker. In a small bowl combine barbecue sauce, honey mustard, and seasoning blend. Pour over ribs. Stir to coat.

2 Cover and cook on low-heat setting for 8 to 10 hours or on high-heat setting for 4 to 5 hours. Transfer ribs to a serving platter. Strain sauce; skim fat from sauce. Drizzle some of the sauce over the ribs. Pass remaining sauce.

Nutrition Facts per serving: 322 cal., 12 g total fat (4 g sat. fat), 94 mg chol., 497 mg sodium, 18 g carbo., 1 g fiber, 29 g pro.
Daily Values: 7% vit. A, 6% vit. C, 4% calcium, 10% iron

Orange Sesame Ribs

This is ribs done the Asian-flavor way. An aromatic, sweet, dark black sauce glazes the meat and drizzles over a side of rice. Sprinkle with toasted sesame seeds for a little crunch.

Prep: 15 minutes Cook: Low 8 hours, High 4 hours Makes: 4 servings

2½ to 3 pounds boneless pork country-style ribs
Nonstick cooking spray
1 10-ounce jar orange marmalade
1 7¼-ounce jar hoisin sauce
3 cloves garlic, minced
1 teaspoon toasted sesame oil
Hot cooked rice (optional)

1 Trim fat from ribs. Lightly coat a large skillet with cooking spray; heat skillet over medium heat. In hot skillet cook ribs until brown. Drain off fat.

2 Place ribs in a 3½- or 4-quart slow cooker. In a medium bowl stir together marmalade, hoisin sauce, garlic, and sesame oil. Pour over ribs in cooker; stir to coat meat with sauce.

3 Cover and cook on low-heat setting for 8 to 10 hours or on high-heat setting for 4 to 5 hours. Transfer meat to a serving platter. Skim fat from sauce. Spoon some of the sauce over the meat. Pass remaining sauce. If desired, serve with hot rice.

Nutrition Facts per serving: 532 cal., 16 g total fat (5 g sat. fat), 101 mg chol., 696 mg sodium, 66 g carbo., 0 g fiber, 33 g pro.
Daily Values: 7% vit. A, 9% vit. C, 9% calcium, 13% iron

Ribs and Sauerkraut

Sauerkraut and onions join the classic apple-and-pork combo for a luscious sweet-salty sensation. Pair this with new potatoes or slices of rye bread.

Prep: 20 minutes Cook: Low 6 hours, High 3 hours Makes: 6 to 8 servings

1 14-ounce can sauerkraut, drained
1 large sweet onion, sliced (2 cups)
2 medium tart cooking apples, peeled, cored, and sliced (about 2 cups)
2 pounds boneless pork country-style ribs
1 cup apple juice

1 In a 4- or 4½-quart slow cooker place sauerkraut, onion, and apples. Top with ribs. Pour apple juice over all.

2 Cover and cook on low-heat setting for 6 to 7 hours or on high-heat setting for 3 to 3½ hours. Serve with a slotted spoon.

Nutrition Facts per serving: 312 cal., 12 g total fat (4 g sat. fat), 96 mg chol., 541 mg sodium, 19 g carbo., 4 g fiber, 30 g pro.
Daily Values: 1% vit. A, 28% vit. C, 7% calcium, 16% iron

Southwest Pork Chops

Control the heat level of this zesty pork main dish by choosing mild, medium, or hot salsa. Garnish with snipped fresh cilantro.

Prep: 15 minutes Cook: Low 5 hours, High 2½ hours; plus 30 minutes on High
Makes: 6 servings

- 6 pork rib chops, cut ¾ inch thick (about 2½ pounds)*
- 1 15½-ounce can Mexican-style or Tex-Mex-style chili beans
- 1¼ cups bottled salsa
- 1 cup frozen whole kernel corn
- 2 cups hot cooked rice
- Snipped fresh cilantro (optional)

1 Trim fat from chops. Place chops in a 3½- or 4-quart slow cooker. Add chili beans and salsa.

2 Cover; cook on low-heat setting for 5 hours or on high-heat setting for 2½ hours.

3 If using low-heat setting, turn to high-heat setting. Stir in corn. Cover and cook 30 minutes more. Serve over hot cooked rice. If desired, sprinkle with cilantro.

***Note:** *To cook all day, substitute 8 boneless pork chops for the 6 rib chops. (When cooked this long, chops with bone may leave bony fragments in the cooked mixture.) Cover and cook on low-heat setting for 9½ hours. Turn to high-heat setting. Stir in corn. Cover and cook 30 minutes more. Serve as above.*

Nutrition Facts per serving: 334 cal., 7 g total fat (2 g sat. fat), 77 mg chol., 716 mg sodium, 34 g carbo., 4 g fiber, 33 g pro.
Daily Values: 5% vit. A, 13% vit. C, 6% calcium, 19% iron

Apple Butter-Sauced Pork Chops

The sauce resembles chunky spiced applesauce, the best possible partner for smoked pork chops. Serve on top of hot cooked couscous.

Prep: 10 minutes Cook: Low 6 hours, High 3 hours Makes: 6 servings

- 6 boneless smoked pork chops (about 1 pound)
- 1 cup apple butter
- 1 teaspoon quick-cooking tapioca
- ½ teaspoon dried sage, crushed
- 2 large red cooking apples
- 3 cups hot cooked couscous (optional)

1 Place chops in a 3½- or 4-quart slow cooker. For sauce, in a small bowl combine apple butter, tapioca, and sage. Pour sauce over the chops. If desired, peel the apples. Core apples and cut into quarters; place on top of chops in cooker.

2 Cover and cook on low-heat setting for 6 to 7 hours or on high-heat setting for 3 to 3½ hours. If desired, serve chops with sauce over hot cooked couscous.

Nutrition Facts per serving: 517 cal., 12 g total fat (4 g sat. fat), 40 mg chol., 641 mg sodium, 87 g carbo., 5 g fiber, 16 g pro.
Daily Values: 4% vit. A, 5% vit. C, 3% calcium, 6% iron

Pork Chops and Corn Bread Stuffing

Try this when you get a craving for Thanksgiving-type fare. Browned chops slow cook over vegetables, soup, and corn bread stuffing mix, yielding a tender, autumn-style meal.

Prep: 20 minutes Cook: Low 5 hours, High 2½ hours Makes: 4 servings

Nonstick cooking spray
4 pork rib chops, cut ¾-inch thick
1 10¾-ounce can condensed golden mushroom or cream of mushroom soup
¼ cup butter or margarine, melted
1 16-ounce package frozen loose-pack broccoli, cauliflower, and carrots
½ of a 16-ounce package corn bread stuffing mix (about 3 cups)

1 Lightly coat a 5½- or 6-quart slow cooker with cooking spray; set aside. Lightly coat a 10-inch skillet with cooking spray; heat over medium heat. In the hot skillet cook chops, half at a time, until brown. Remove chops from skillet; set aside.

2 In a very large bowl stir together the soup and melted butter. Add frozen vegetables and stuffing mix; stir to combine. Transfer mixture to prepared cooker. Arrange chops on top of stuffing mixture.

3 Cover and cook on low-heat setting for 5 to 6 hours or on high-heat setting for 2½ to 3 hours.

Nutrition Facts per serving: 558 cal., 22 g total fat (10 g sat. fat), 89 mg chol., 1,533 mg sodium, 56 g carbo., 7 g fiber, 30 g pro.
Daily Values: 66% vit. A, 47% vit. C, 9% calcium, 20% iron

Pork Chops with Orange-Dijon Sauce

Dried thyme, mustard, and orange marmalade season this boneless pork chop dinner. Serve with steamed broccoli and rice pilaf.

Prep: 15 minutes Cook: Low 6 hours, High 3 hours Makes: 6 servings

- 6 boneless pork sirloin chops, cut 1-inch thick
- Salt and black pepper
- ½ teaspoon dried thyme, crushed
- 1 cup orange marmalade
- ⅓ cup Dijon-style mustard
- ¼ cup water

1 Sprinkle both sides of chops lightly with salt and pepper. Sprinkle chops with thyme. Place chops in a 3½- or 4-quart slow cooker. In a small bowl combine orange marmalade and mustard. Remove 2 tablespoons of the mixture; cover and refrigerate. Combine remaining marmalade mixture and water. Pour over chops.

2 Cover and cook on low-heat setting for 6 to 7 hours or on high-heat setting for 3 to 3½ hours. Transfer chops to a serving platter; discard cooking liquid. Spread reserved marmalade mixture over chops.

Nutrition Facts per serving: 409 cal., 15 g total fat (5 g sat. fat), 166 mg chol., 212 mg sodium, 9 g carbo., 1 g fiber, 56 g pro.
Daily Values: 1% vit. A, 5% vit. C, 5% calcium, 14% iron

Choucroute Garni

Choucroute is a French word that refers to sauerkraut that's garnished with meats—in this case, smoked pork and sausage—and potatoes. Serve with a variety of mustards.

Prep: 10 minutes Cook: Low 8 hours, High 4 hours Makes: 8 servings

1 14- to 15-ounce can Bavarian-style sauerkraut (with caraway seeds), rinsed and drained
1 pound Yukon gold potatoes, quartered
1 pound cooked smoked boneless pork chops, halved crosswise
1 pound cooked bratwurst, halved crosswise, or cooked, smoked Polish sausage, cut into 3-inch lengths
1 12-ounce bottle or can beer

1 In a 4½- to 6-quart slow cooker place sauerkraut and potatoes. Top with pork chops and bratwurst. Pour beer over all

2 Cover and cook on low-heat setting for 8 to 9 hours or on high-heat setting for 4 to 4½ hours.

Nutrition Facts per serving: 311 cal., 17 g total fat (6 g sat. fat), 64 mg chol., 2,158 mg sodium, 16 g carbo., 1 g fiber, 19 g pro.
Daily Values: 15% vit. C, 3% calcium, 9% iron

Ham and Potatoes au Gratin

This golden yellow casserole is like macaroni and cheese without the macaroni. Kids will like its rosy ham, soft potatoes, and rich cheese flavor. Roasted red peppers add flavor and color.

Prep: 15 minutes Cook: Low 7 hours, High 3½ hours Makes: 6 servings

Nonstick cooking spray
2 5½-ounce packages dry au gratin potato mix
2 cups diced cooked ham
¼ cup bottled roasted red sweet pepper, drained and chopped
3 cups water
1 10¾-ounce can condensed cheddar cheese soup

1 Lightly coat a 3½- or 4-quart slow cooker with cooking spray. Place au gratin potato mixes with contents of seasoning packets, the ham, and roasted red pepper in the prepared cooker. In a large bowl stir together water and soup. Pour over potato mixture in cooker.

2 Cover and cook on low-heat setting for 7 to 8 hours or on high-heat setting for 3½ to 4 hours.

Nutrition Facts per serving: 255 cal., 7 g total fat (3 g sat. fat), 29 mg chol., 2,087 mg sodium, 45 g carbo., 3 g fiber, 15 g pro.
Daily Values: 11% vit. A, 42% vit. C, 21% calcium, 8% iron

Slow Cooker Lasagna

Lasagna in a slow cooker? You bet. Here sweet Italian sausage is layered with noodles, cheeses, and pasta sauce. Plan a light dessert: apple or pear slices and candied nuts.

Prep: 20 minutes Cook: Low 4 hours, High 2 hours Stand: 15 minutes Makes: 8 to 10 servings

- Nonstick cooking spray
- 1 pound bulk sweet Italian sausage
- 1 26-ounce jar chunky tomato, basil, and cheese pasta sauce
- ¾ cup water
- 12 no-boil lasagna noodles
- 1 15-ounce container ricotta cheese
- 1 8-ounce package shredded Italian blend cheese

1 Lightly coat a 3½- or 4-quart slow cooker with cooking spray; set aside. In a large skillet cook sausage until brown. Drain off fat. Stir in pasta sauce and water.

2 Place ½ cup of the meat mixture in the bottom of the prepared cooker. Layer 4 of the noodles (break noodles to fit) on top the meat mixture. Top with one-third of the ricotta cheese, one-third of the remaining meat mixture, and one-third of the shredded cheese. Repeat layers twice, starting with noodles and ending with meat mixture. Set aside the remaining cheese.

3 Cover and cook on low-heat setting for 4 to 6 hours or on high-heat setting for 2 to 3 hours. Uncover; sprinkle with remaining shredded cheese. Let stand about 15 minutes before serving.

Nutrition Facts per serving: 497 cal., 30 g total fat (14 g sat. fat), 87 mg chol., 909 mg sodium, 26 g carbo., 1 g fiber, 26 g pro.
Daily Values: 11% vit. A, 8% vit. C, 32% calcium, 8% iron

Mexican Lasagna

The layers are tender; the flavor is full and zesty. Best of all, there's no messy scooping necessary—after standing, this lasagna holds a soft-cut edge.

Prep: 25 minutes Cook: Low 3 hours Stand: 15 minutes Makes: 8 servings

Nonstick cooking spray
1½ pounds bulk pork sausage
9 6-inch corn tortillas
1 11-ounce can whole kernel corn with sweet peppers, drained
2 cups shredded taco cheese (8 ounces)
1 19-ounce can enchilada sauce

1 Lightly coat a 3½- or 4-quart slow cooker with cooking spray; set aside. In a large skillet cook sausage until brown; drain off fat.

2 Place 3 of the tortillas in the bottom of the prepared cooker, overlapping as necessary. Top with half of the corn and half of the sausage. Sprinkle with ½ cup of the cheese. Pour about ¾ cup of the enchilada sauce over layers in cooker. Repeat with 3 more tortillas, remaining corn, and remaining sausage. Sprinkle with ½ cup of the cheese. Pour ¾ cup enchilada sauce over cheese. Top with remaining 3 tortillas, remaining 1 cup cheese, and remaining enchilada sauce.

3 Cover and cook on low-heat setting for 3 to 4 hours. Remove liner from cooker or turn off cooker. Let stand, covered, 15 minutes before serving.

Nutrition Facts per serving: 512 cal., 34 g total fat (15 g sat. fat), 71 mg chol., 1,082 mg sodium, 27 g carbo., 3 g fiber, 18 g pro.
Daily Values: 17% vit. A, 2% vit. C, 22% calcium, 5% iron

Pizza by the Yard

Toasted Italian bread makes an easy crust for your pizza. Serve it with salad for supper or on its own as a hearty party appetizer. Sliced olives add extra flavor.

Prep: 25 minutes Cook: Low 5 hours, High 2½ hours Makes: 8 servings

- 2 pounds bulk Italian sausage
- 1 26-ounce jar garlic and mushroom pasta sauce
- 2 large green and/or red sweet peppers, chopped
- 1 1-pound loaf Italian bread, split lengthwise and toasted*
- 1 8-ounce package shredded pizza cheese

1 In a large skillet cook sausage over medium heat until brown. Drain off fat. In a 3½- or 4-quart slow cooker combine sausage, pasta sauce, and sweet pepper.

2 Cover and cook on low-heat setting for 5 to 6 hours or on high-heat setting for 2½ to 3 hours. Spoon sausage mixture over toasted bread. Sprinkle with cheese.

*Note: *To toast bread, place bread, cut sides up, on a baking sheet. Broil 3 to 4 inches from heat for 3 to 4 minutes or until toasted.*

Nutrition Facts per serving: 699 cal., 46 g total fat (17 g sat. fat), 106 mg chol., 1,935 mg sodium, 38 g carbo., 4 g fiber, 30 g pro. Daily Values: 16% vit. A, 57% vit. C, 30% calcium, 22% iron

Mediterranean Lamb Shanks

Pesto sauce captures the flavor of the Mediterranean sun and summer gardens. If you like, serve the lamb with couscous sprinkled with shredded lemon peel and snipped parsley.

Prep: 10 minutes Cook: Low 7 hours, High 3½ hours Makes: 6 servings

- 1 16-ounce package frozen loose-pack Italian vegetables (zucchini, carrots, cauliflower, lima beans, Italian beans)
- 1 14½-ounce can diced tomatoes with basil, garlic, and oregano, undrained
- 1 14-ounce can chicken broth
- 3 to 3½ pounds meaty lamb shanks
- ½ cup refrigerated basil pesto

1. In a 5- to 6-quart slow cooker combine frozen vegetables, undrained tomatoes, and chicken broth. Top with meat. Spoon pesto over the meat.

2. Cover and cook on low-heat setting for 7 to 9 hours or on high-heat setting for 3½ to 4½ hours. Using a slotted spoon, transfer meat and vegetables to a serving platter.

Nutrition Facts per serving: 314 cal., 16 g total fat (1 g sat. fat), 66 mg chol., 884 mg sodium, 14 g carbo., 2 g fiber, 25 g pro.
Daily Values: 53% vit. A, 17% vit. C, 7% calcium, 15% iron

Lamb Curry

Curry powder imparts a sunny color and a spicy taste to lamb and veggies. Sprinkle each serving with coconut, raisins, and sunflower seeds for an authentic Indian classic.

Prep: 10 minutes Cook: Low 7 hours, High 3½ hours Makes: 10 servings

- 2 pounds lamb stew meat
- 1 16-ounce package frozen loose-pack broccoli, cauliflower, and carrots
- 2 10¾-ounce cans condensed cream of onion soup
- ½ cup water
- 2 to 3 teaspoons curry powder
- 5 cups hot cooked rice

1 In a 3½- or 4-quart slow cooker combine meat, frozen vegetables, soup, water, and curry powder.

2 Cover and cook on low-heat setting for 7 to 8 hours or on high-heat setting for 3½ to 4 hours. Serve over hot cooked rice.

Nutrition Facts per serving: 295 cal., 7 g total fat (2 g sat. fat), 68 mg chol., 727 mg sodium, 33 g carbo., 2 g fiber, 23 g pro.
Daily Values: 22% vit. A, 9% vit. C, 5% calcium, 18% iron

Greek Cabbage Rolls

This Mediterranean classic features the bold flavors the region is known for. Top with feta cheese for additional tang.

Prep: 30 minutes Cook: Low 6 hours, High 3 hours Makes: 5 servings (2 rolls per serving)

1 large head green cabbage
1 pound ground lamb or lean ground beef
2 teaspoons Greek seasoning
1 26-ounce jar mushroom and ripe olive tomato pasta sauce
1 cup cooked rice
Crumbled feta cheese (optional)

1 Remove 10 large outer leaves from the cabbage.* In a Dutch oven cook cabbage leaves in boiling water for 3 to 4 minutes or just until leaves are limp. Drain cabbage leaves. Trim the thick rib from the center of each leaf. Set leaves aside. Shred 2 cups of the remaining cabbage; set aside. (Wrap and chill remaining cabbage for another use.)

2 In a large skillet cook meat with Greek seasoning until meat is brown; drain off fat. Add the shredded cabbage, ½ cup of the pasta sauce, and the rice; stir to combine. Evenly divide the lamb mixture among the 10 cabbage leaves. Fold sides of leaves over filling and roll up. Place cabbage rolls in a 3½- or 4-quart slow cooker. Top with remaining pasta sauce.

3 Cover and cook on low-heat setting 6 to 7 hours or on high-heat setting for 3 to 3½ hours. If desired, top with crumbled feta cheese.

***Note:** *To easily remove the cabbage leaves, place the cabbage head in boiling water for 2 to 3 minutes to loosen the outer leaves.*

Nutrition Facts per serving: 323 cal., 14 g total fat (6 g sat. fat), 61 mg chol., 707 mg sodium, 28 g carbo., 8 g fiber, 22 g pro.
Daily Values: 4% vit. A, 194% vit. C, 13% calcium, 14% iron

4

Main Dishes Without Meat

Taco-Style Black Beans and Hominy

Taco seasoning is the key to revving up the rich and velvety bean-grain mix. Serve it in taco shells for dinner or mini taco shells for a party appetizer or snack.

Prep: 15 minutes Cook: Low 7 hours, High 3½ hours Makes: 9 servings

- Nonstick cooking spray
- 2 15- to 15½-ounce cans black beans, rinsed and drained
- 2 14½- to 15½-ounce cans golden hominy, drained
- 1¼ cups water
- 1 10¾-ounce can condensed cream of mushroom soup
- ½ of a 1¼-ounce package (1½ tablespoons) taco seasoning mix
- 18 taco shells
- Sliced green onions, chopped tomato, and/or shredded lettuce (optional)

1. Coat a 3½- or 4-quart slow cooker with cooking spray. In the prepared cooker stir together the beans, hominy, water, soup, and taco seasoning.

2. Cover and cook on low-heat setting for 7 to 8 hours or on high-heat setting for 3½ to 4 hours.

3. To serve, spoon into taco shells. If desired, sprinkle with sliced green onions, tomato, and/or lettuce.

Nutrition Facts per serving: 317 cal., 10 g total fat (2 g sat. fat), 0 mg chol., 1,001 mg sodium, 52 g carbo., 11 g fiber, 12 g pro.
Daily Values: 2% vit. A, 1% vit. C, 11% calcium, 16% iron

Bean-and-Rice-Stuffed Peppers

Cheese, chili beans, and rice come straight from the cooker, neatly packaged in sweet peppers. Use a mix of green, red, and yellow peppers for a festive presentation.

Prep: 15 minutes Cook: Low 6 hours, High 3 hours Makes: 4 servings

- 4 small to medium green, red, or yellow sweet peppers
- 1 cup cooked converted rice
- 1 15-ounce can chili beans with chili gravy
- 4 ounces Monterey Jack cheese, shredded (1 cup)
- 1 15-ounce can chunky tomato sauce with onion, celery, and green sweet pepper

1 Remove tops of sweet peppers; scoop out membranes and seeds. Set aside. For filling, in a bowl stir together the rice, beans, and ½ cup of the cheese. Spoon filling into peppers. Pour tomato sauce into bottom of a 5- to 6-quart slow cooker. Arrange stuffed peppers, filling side up, in the cooker.

2 Cover and cook on low-heat setting for 6 to 6½ hours or on high-heat setting for 3 to 3½ hours.

3 To serve, transfer peppers to serving plates. Spoon tomato sauce over peppers and sprinkle with remaining cheese.

Nutrition Facts per serving: 323 cal., 11 g total fat (5 g sat. fat), 25 mg chol., 918 mg sodium, 41 g carbo., 9 g fiber, 16 g pro.
Daily Values: 86% vit. A, 206% vit. C, 34% calcium, 16% iron

Stuffed Cabbage Rolls

Your choice of black or red beans and brown rice stand in for the filling of ground beef and rice that's typical of this classic.

Prep: 25 minutes Cook: Low 6 hours, High 3 hours Makes: 4 servings (2 rolls per serving)

- ½ cup instant brown rice
- 1 large head green cabbage (about 2 pounds)
- 1 15- to 16-ounce can black beans or red kidney beans, rinsed and drained
- ½ cup chopped onion (1 medium)
- 1 26- or 28-ounce jar chunky tomato pasta sauce or meatless spaghetti sauce
- Shredded cheddar cheese (optional)

1 In a small saucepan bring ½ cup water to boiling. Stir in uncooked rice. Reduce heat; cover and simmer for 10 minutes or until water is absorbed. Remove from heat; set aside.

2 Meanwhile, remove 8 large outer leaves from the cabbage.* In a 4-quart Dutch oven cook cabbage leaves, covered, in boiling water for 4 to 5 minutes or just until leaves are limp. Drain cabbage leaves. Trim the thick rib in the center of each leaf. Set leaves aside. Shred 4 cups of the remaining cabbage; place shredded cabbage in a 3½- or 4-quart slow cooker. (Wrap and chill remaining cabbage for another use.)

3 In a medium bowl combine beans, cooked rice, onion, and ½ cup of the pasta sauce. Evenly divide the bean mixture among the 8 cabbage leaves, using about ⅓ cup per leaf. Fold sides of leaf over filling and roll up. Pour about half of the remaining pasta sauce over shredded cabbage in cooker. Stir to mix. Place cabbage rolls on the shredded cabbage. Top with remaining pasta sauce.

4 Cover and cook on low-heat setting for 6 to 7 hours or on high-heat setting for 3 to 3½ hours. Carefully remove the cooked cabbage rolls and serve with the shredded cabbage mixture. If desired, sprinkle with cheddar cheese.

***Note:** *To easily remove the cabbage leaves, place the cabbage head in boiling water for 2 to 3 minutes to loosen the outer leaves.*

Nutrition Facts per serving: 332 cal., 6 g total fat (1 g sat. fat), 0 mg chol., 1,042 mg sodium, 64 g carbo., 15 g fiber, 15 g pro.
Daily Values: 41% vit. A, 112% vit. C, 17% calcium, 22% iron

Greek-Seasoned Lentils

Classic Greek seasonings impart a zesty, fresh flavor that is pleasing with lentils. Eat them on toasted pita wedges with a sprinkle of sliced green onion and chopped tomato.

Prep: 15 minutes Cook: Low 6 hours, High 3 hours Makes: 6 to 8 servings

2 cups dry lentils
Nonstick cooking spray
2 cups purchased shredded carrots
1 cup chopped onion (1 large)
3 14-ounce cans vegetable broth
2 teaspoons Greek seasoning

1 Rinse lentils. Drain well. Lightly coat a 3½- to 5-quart slow cooker with cooking spray. In the prepared slow cooker combine the lentils, carrots, onion, vegetable broth, and Greek seasoning.

2 Cover and cook on low-heat setting for 6 to 7 hours or on high-heat setting for 3 to 3½ hours. Serve lentils with a slotted spoon.

Nutrition Facts per serving: 260 cal., 2 g total fat (0 g sat. fat), 0 mg chol., 874 mg sodium, 45 g carbo., 21 g fiber, 20 g pro.
Daily Values: 209% vit. A, 12% vit. C, 4% calcium, 27% iron

White Beans with Dried Tomatoes

Soft white beans in vegetable broth absorb the flavors of garlic, dried tomatoes, and shaved Asiago cheese. Partner with toasted, buttered baguette slices for a complementary crunch.

Prep: 15 minutes Cook: Low 6 hours, High 3½ hours; plus 15 minutes on High Makes: 6 servings

- 3 15- to 19-ounce cans white kidney beans (cannellini beans), rinsed and drained
- 1 14-ounce can vegetable broth
- 3 cloves garlic, minced
- 1 7-ounce jar oil-packed dried tomatoes, drained and chopped
- 4 ounces shaved Asiago or Parmesan cheese (1 cup)
- ⅓ cup pine nuts, toasted* (optional)

1 In a 3½- or 4-quart slow cooker combine beans, vegetable broth, and garlic.

2 Cover and cook on low-heat setting for 6 to 8 hours or on high-heat setting for 3½ to 4 hours. If using low-heat setting, turn to high-heat setting. Stir in tomatoes. Cover and cook for 15 minutes more or until tomatoes are heated through.

3 To serve, top each serving with cheese. If desired, top with pine nuts.

***Note:** *To toast nuts, spread nuts in a single layer in a shallow baking pan. Bake in a 350°F oven for 5 to 10 minutes or until light golden brown, watching carefully and stirring once or twice so the nuts don't burn.*

Nutrition Facts per serving: 285 cal., 13 g total fat (5 g sat. fat), 20 mg chol., 901 mg sodium, 38 g carbo., 12 g fiber, 19 g pro.
Daily Values: 10% vit. A, 57% vit. C, 23% calcium, 18% iron

Curried Couscous with Vegetables

This recipe is a hodgepodge of flavor and texture: savory-sweet with zing from jalapeño peppers and a subtle crunch by way of almonds.

Prep: 15 minutes Cook: Low 4 hours, High 2 hours Stand: 5 minutes Makes: 8 servings

- 1 large onion, cut into thin wedges
- 2 cups coarsely chopped yellow summer squash and/or zucchini
- 2 14½-ounce cans diced tomatoes with jalapeño peppers, undrained
- 2 cups water
- 2 5.7-ounce packages curry-flavored couscous mix
- 1 cup chopped toasted, slivered almonds*
- ½ cup raisins (optional)

1 In a 3½- or 4-quart slow cooker combine onion, summer squash, undrained tomatoes, water, and seasoning packets from couscous mixes.

2 Cover and cook on low-heat setting for 4 to 6 hours or on high-heat setting for 2 to 3 hours. Stir in couscous. Turn off cooker. Cover and let stand 5 minutes. Fluff couscous mixture with a fork.

3 To serve, sprinkle each serving with almonds and, if desired, raisins.

***Note:** *To toast nuts, spread nuts in a single layer in a shallow baking pan. Bake in a 350°F oven for 5 to 10 minutes or until light golden brown, watching carefully and stirring once or twice so the nuts don't burn.*

Nutrition Facts per serving: 280 cal., 9 g total fat (1 g sat. fat), 0 mg chol., 842 mg sodium, 43 g carbo., 6 g fiber, 10 g pro.
Daily Values: 18% vit. A, 20% vit. C, 9% calcium, 13% iron

Beans with Pesto

Tender beans and pilaf get sharp with Parmesan and pesto. Enjoy it straight up or roll a serving in a whole wheat tortilla.

Prep: 15 minutes Cook: Low 4 hours, High 2 hours; plus 20 minutes on High
Makes: 6 to 8 servings

- 2 15-ounce cans pinto beans, black beans, or garbanzo beans, rinsed and drained
- 4 cups water
- 1 large red sweet pepper, chopped
- ½ cup refrigerated basil pesto
- 2 7.2-ounce packages herb-seasoned rice pilaf mix
- ½ cup finely shredded Parmesan cheese (2 ounces)

1 In a 3½- or 4-quart slow cooker combine beans, water, sweet pepper, pesto, and seasoning packets from rice mixes.

2 Cover and cook on low-heat setting for 4 to 5 hours or on high-heat setting for 2 to 2½ hours. If using low-heat setting, turn to high-heat setting. Stir in rice mix. Cover and cook 20 minutes more. Top each serving with Parmesan cheese.

Nutrition Facts per serving: 548 cal., 18 g total fat (2 g sat. fat), 11 mg chol., 1,798 mg sodium, 79 g carbo., 9 g fiber, 21 g pro.
Daily Values: 30% vit. A, 70% vit. C, 18% calcium, 19% iron

Sweet-and-Sour Tofu

Cubes of teriyaki-flavored tofu are soft and pretty in a sweet-and-sour sauce with crunchy sweet peppers and water chestnuts. Serve this colorful dish over hot cooked rice.

Prep: 15 minutes Cook: Low 4 hours, High 2 hours Makes: 4 to 6 servings

- 2 16-ounce packages frozen loose-pack pepper stir-fry vegetables (yellow, green, and red sweet peppers and onions)
- 1 9-ounce jar sweet-and-sour sauce
- 1 8-ounce can sliced water chestnuts, drained
- 1 6½- to 7-ounce package baked or smoked teriyaki-flavored tofu, drained and cut into ½-inch pieces
- 2 cups hot cooked rice

1 In a 3½- or 4-quart slow cooker combine stir-fry vegetables, sweet-and-sour sauce, and water chestnuts.

2 Cover and cook on low-heat setting for 4 to 4½ hours or on high-heat setting for 2 to 2¼ hours. Stir in tofu. Serve over hot cooked rice.

Nutrition Facts per serving: 318 cal., 7 g total fat (1 g sat. fat), 0 mg chol., 597 mg sodium, 73 g carbo., 4 g fiber, 13 g pro.
Daily Values: 27% vit. A, 142% vit. C, 22% calcium, 18% iron

Red Beans over Spanish Rice

Tender red beans go from tame to sassy when mixed with cumin. Slice lime wedges to serve on the side: A spritz of citrus is a nice twist.

Prep: 25 minutes Cook: Low 10 hours, High 5 hours Stand: 1 hour Makes: 6 to 8 servings

- 2 cups dry red beans or dry red kidney beans
- 5 cups water
- Nonstick cooking spray
- 4 cups water
- 2½ cups chopped onion
- 1 tablespoon bottled minced garlic (6 cloves)
- 1 tablespoon ground cumin
- 1 6¾-ounce package Spanish rice mix
- Lime wedges (optional)

1 Rinse beans. In a large saucepan combine dry beans and the 5 cups water. Bring to boiling; reduce heat. Simmer, uncovered, for 10 minutes. Remove from heat. Cover and let stand for 1 hour. (Or place beans in the 5 cups water in saucepan. Cover; let soak in a cool place for 6 to 8 hours or overnight.) Drain and rinse beans.

2 Lightly coat a 3½- or 4-quart slow cooker with cooking spray. In the prepared cooker place beans, the 4 cups water, onion, garlic, and cumin.

3 Cover and cook on low-heat setting for 10 to 11 hours or on high-heat setting for 5 to 5½ hours. Prepare the rice mix according to package directions. Remove beans from cooker using a slotted spoon. Serve beans over cooked rice. If desired, spoon some of the cooking liquid from the cooker and a squeeze of lime juice over beans and rice.

Nutrition Facts per serving: 344 cal., 1 g total fat (0 g sat. fat), 0 mg chol., 450 mg sodium, 68 g carbo., 17 g fiber, 19 g pro.
Daily Values: 6% vit. A, 14% vit. C, 17% calcium, 34% iron

Vegetable-Rice Casserole

If your goal is to serve a meatless supper, accompany this cheesy main dish with a tossed green salad and serve fruit for dessert.

Prep: 15 minutes Cook: Low 3½ hours Makes: 4 servings

- 1 16-ounce package frozen loose-pack cauliflower, broccoli, and carrots
- 1 15-ounce can garbanzo beans, rinsed and drained
- 1 10¾-ounce can condensed cream of celery or cream of mushroom soup
- 1 cup instant white rice
- ½ of a 15-ounce jar (about 1 cup) process cheese sauce
- 1 cup water

1 In a 3½- or 4-quart slow cooker place frozen vegetables and beans. In a bowl combine soup, uncooked rice, cheese sauce, and water. Pour over the vegetables.

2 Cover and cook on low-heat setting for 3½ to 4½ hours or until vegetables and rice are tender. Stir well before serving.

Nutrition Facts per serving: 436 cal., 17 g total fat (10 g sat. fat), 34 mg chol., 1,923 mg sodium, 52 g carbo., 9 g fiber, 17 g pro.
Daily Values: 60% vit. A, 47% vit. C, 24% calcium, 14% iron

Cajun-Seasoned Vegetarian Gumbo

Spunky Cajun seasoning, velvety black beans, and colorful vegetables keep this lively, loaded gumbo interesting. There's plenty of sauce to flavor accompanying rice.

Prep: 10 minutes Cook: Low 6 hours, High 3 hours Makes: 6 servings

- 2 15-ounce cans black beans, rinsed and drained
- 1 28-ounce can diced tomatoes, undrained
- 1 16-ounce package frozen loose-pack pepper stir-fry vegetables (yellow, green, and red sweet peppers, and onions)
- 2 cups frozen cut okra
- 2 to 3 teaspoons Cajun seasoning
- Hot cooked white or brown rice (optional)

1 In a 3½- to 4½-quart slow cooker combine beans, undrained tomatoes, stir-fry vegetables, okra, and Cajun seasoning.

2 Cover and cook on low-heat setting for 6 to 8 hours or on high-heat setting for 3 to 4 hours. If desired, serve over hot cooked rice.

Nutrition Facts per serving: 153 cal., 0 g total fat (0 g sat. fat), 0 mg chol., 639 mg sodium, 31 g carbo., 10 g fiber, 12 g pro.
Daily Values: 32% vit. A, 63% vit. C, 12% calcium, 28% iron

Cheesy Tortellini Casserole

Seasoned tomatoes and marinara sauce flavor the cheese tortellini. Ground sausage-style meat substitute (a soy product) boosts the total grams of protein.

Prep: 5 minutes Cook: Low 7 hours, High 3½ hours; plus 15 minutes on Low Stand: 10 minutes
Makes: 8 servings

Nonstick cooking spray
2 15-ounce containers refrigerated marinara sauce
2 14½-ounce cans diced tomatoes with basil, oregano, and garlic, undrained
1 12-ounce package frozen cooked and crumbled ground sausage-style meat substitute (soy protein)
1 9-ounce package refrigerated cheese-filled tortellini
1 cup shredded mozzarella cheese (4 ounces)

1 Lightly coat a 3½- or 4-quart slow cooker with cooking spray. In prepared cooker stir together the marinara sauce, undrained tomatoes, and meat substitute.

2 Cover and cook on low-heat setting for 7 to 8 hours or on high-heat setting for 3½ to 4 hours.

3 If using high-heat setting, turn to low-heat setting. Stir in tortellini. Cover and cook for 15 to 20 minutes more or until tortellini are tender. Sprinkle with mozzarella cheese. Let stand, covered, for 10 minutes or until cheese is melted.

Nutrition Facts per serving: 298 cal., 10 g total fat (3 g sat. fat), 23 mg chol., 1,377 mg sodium, 34 g carbo., 2 g fiber, 21 g pro.
Daily Values: 15% vit. A, 12% vit. C, 24% calcium, 17% iron

Pasta with Sweet Beans

Rosemary's garden scent and flavor reign over this sweet edamame bean-Alfredo sauce mixture served over linguine.

Prep: 10 minutes Cook: Low 4 hours, High 2 hours Makes: 4 servings

- 1 12-ounce package frozen sweet soybeans (edamame), thawed (2¾ cups)
- 2 cups purchased shredded carrots
- 1 16-ounce jar Alfredo pasta sauce
- 1 teaspoon dried rosemary, crushed
- 8 ounces dried linguine
- Finely shredded Parmesan (optional)

1 In a 3½- or 4-quart slow cooker combine soybeans, carrots, Alfredo pasta sauce, and rosemary.

2 Cover and cook on low-heat setting for 4 to 5 hours or on high-heat setting for 2 to 2½ hours. Cook pasta according to package directions; drain. Serve bean mixture over hot cooked pasta. If desired, sprinkle with Parmesan cheese.

Nutrition Facts per serving: 720 cal., 42 g total fat (1 g sat. fat), 57 mg chol., 448 mg sodium, 64 g carbo., 7 g fiber, 25 g pro.
Daily Values: 312% vit. A, 36% vit. C, 17% calcium, 28% iron

Garlic-Artichoke Pasta

Herb-infused tomatoes tango with garlic, artichokes, and cream—a dance that results in a sauce with Mediterranean flair. Garnish with your favorite cheese and sliced olives.

Prep: 15 minutes Cook: Low 6 hours, High 3 hours Stand: 5 minutes Makes: 6 servings

Nonstick cooking spray
3 14½-ounce cans diced tomatoes with basil, oregano, and garlic, undrained
2 14-ounce cans artichoke hearts, drained and quartered
1 tablespoon bottled minced garlic (6 cloves)
½ cup whipping cream
12 ounces dried linguine, fettuccine, or other favorite pasta
Sliced pimiento-stuffed green olives and/or sliced pitted ripe olives (optional)
Crumbled feta cheese or finely shredded Parmesan cheese (optional)

1 Coat a 3½- or 4-quart slow cooker with cooking spray. Drain 2 of the cans of diced tomatoes (do not drain remaining can). In the prepared cooker combine drained and undrained tomatoes, artichoke hearts, and garlic.

2 Cover and cook on low-heat setting for 6 to 8 hours or on high-heat setting for 3 to 4 hours. Stir in whipping cream; let stand about 5 minutes to heat through.

3 Cook pasta according to package directions; drain. Serve sauce over hot cooked pasta. If desired, top with olives and/or cheese.

Nutrition Facts per serving: 403 cal., 8 g total fat (5 g sat. fat), 27 mg chol., 1,513 mg sodium, 68 g carbo., 7 g fiber, 13 g pro.
Daily Values: 35% vit. A, 30% vit. C, 20% calcium, 45% iron

Eggplant Sauce with Whole Wheat Pasta

Here's a meatless dish you can really sink your teeth into. The chunky eggplant sauce is rich in onions, garlic, and olives.

Prep: 15 minutes Cook: Low 3 hours Makes: 6 servings

Nonstick cooking spray
1 medium eggplant, cut into 1-inch pieces (5½ cups)
1 large onion, cut into thin wedges
1 2¼-ounce can sliced pitted ripe olives, drained
1 28-ounce jar roasted garlic pasta sauce
12 ounces dried whole wheat penne or rotini pasta
Shredded Parmesan cheese (optional)

1 Coat a 3½- or 4-quart slow cooker with cooking spray. In the prepared cooker combine the eggplant, onion, and olives. Stir in pasta sauce.

2 Cover and cook on low-heat setting for 3 to 4 hours. Cook pasta according to package directions; drain. Serve sauce over hot cooked pasta. If desired, sprinkle with Parmesan cheese.

Nutrition Facts per serving: 316 cal., 4 g total fat (0 g sat. fat), 0 mg chol., 512 mg sodium, 60 g carbo., 8 g fiber, 10 g pro.
Daily Values: 11% vit. A, 15% vit. C, 11% calcium, 23% iron

Creamy Tomato-Broccoli Sauce with Pasta

Bearing the red, white, and green of the Italian flag, this pasta dish gets a lively edge from parma rosa sauce mix. The sauce is creamy and the broccoli chunks crisp-tender.

Prep: 15 minutes Cook: Low 6 hours, High 3 hours; plus 15 minutes on High
Makes: 8 to 10 servings

Nonstick cooking spray
2 14½-ounce cans diced tomatoes with basil, oregano, and garlic, undrained
2 10¾-ounce cans condensed cream of mushroom soup
1 1.3-ounce envelope parma rosa pasta sauce mix
1 cup water
1 16-ounce package frozen cut broccoli
16 ounces dried penne or mostaccioli pasta

1 Coat a 3½- or 4-quart slow cooker with cooking spray. In a large bowl combine the undrained tomatoes, soup, sauce mix, and water. Pour into prepared cooker.

2 Cover and cook on low-heat setting for 6 to 8 hours or on high-heat setting for 3 to 4 hours. If using low-heat setting, turn to high-heat setting. Stir in broccoli; cover and cook on high-heat setting for 15 minutes or until broccoli is crisp-tender.

3 Cook pasta according to package directions; drain. Toss pasta with sauce. Spoon into bowls to serve.

Nutrition Facts per serving: 365 cal., 7 g total fat (2 g sat. fat), 1 mg chol., 1,270 mg sodium, 62 g carbo., 4 g fiber, 12 g pro.
Daily Values: 26% vit. A, 54% vit. C, 12% calcium, 21% iron

Vegetarian Chili

Lots of beans and crumbled meat substitute mingle with onions, tomatoes, and chili powder. If you need to stretch the number of servings, spoon it over couscous or corn bread wedges.

Prep: 10 minutes Cook: Low 6 hours, High 3 hours Makes: 6 servings

Nonstick cooking spray
2 15-ounce cans chili beans with chili gravy
2 14½-ounce cans Mexican-style stewed tomatoes, undrained
2 cups frozen cooked and crumbled ground meat substitute (soy protein)
1 cup chopped onion (1 large)
1 tablespoon chili powder

1 Lightly coat a 3½- or 4-quart slow cooker with cooking spray. In the prepared cooker combine the undrained beans, undrained tomatoes, ground meat substitute, onion, and chili powder.

2 Cover and cook on low-heat setting for 6 to 7 hours or on high-heat setting for 3 to 3½ hours. To serve, ladle into bowls.

Nutrition Facts per serving: 230 cal., 2 g total fat (0 g sat. fat), 0 mg chol., 959 mg sodium, 40 g carbo., 13 g fiber, 17 g pro.
Daily Values: 9% vit. A, 23% vit. C, 12% calcium, 17% iron

Vegetable Chili Medley

A medley of beans, corn, and tomatoes combines in this spicy chili. Choose the diced tomatoes with green chile peppers if you like fiery meals.

Prep: 10 minutes Cook: Low 6 hours, High 3 hours Makes: 6 servings

2 14½-ounce cans diced tomatoes or diced tomatoes and green chile peppers, undrained
2 15-ounce cans kidney, garbanzo, and/or black beans, rinsed and drained
1 15-ounce can tomato sauce
1 cup water
1 10-ounce package frozen whole kernel corn
1 1¼-ounce envelope chili seasoning mix
Shredded cheddar cheese (optional)

1 In a 3½- to 4½-quart slow cooker combine undrained tomatoes, beans, tomato sauce, water, corn, and chili seasoning mix.

2 Cover and cook on low-heat setting for 6 to 7 hours or on high-heat setting for 3 to 3½ hours. Ladle into bowls. If desired, top with cheddar cheese.

Nutrition Facts per serving: 218 cal., 1 g total fat (0 g sat. fat), 0 mg chol., 1,346 mg sodium, 46 g carbo., 10 g fiber, 13 g pro.
Daily Values: 6% vit. A, 33% vit. C, 9% calcium, 18% iron

Tortellini Soup Alfredo

What to eat when comfort food sounds too heavy and soup sounds too light? This soup, with its substantial pasta and creamy sauce, makes an attractive in-between solution.

Prep: 15 minutes Cook: Low 5 hours, High 2½ hours; plus 1 hour on High
Makes: 4 main-dish servings (7½ cups)

- 1 28-ounce jar or two 16-ounce jars Alfredo pasta sauce
- 2 14-ounce cans vegetable broth
- ½ cup chopped onion
- 1 2-ounce jar sliced pimientos, drained and chopped
- 1 6- to 8-ounce package dried cheese-filled tortellini

1 In a 3½- or 4-quart slow cooker combine Alfredo pasta sauce, vegetable broth, onion, and pimientos.

2 Cover and cook on low-heat setting for 5 to 6 hours or on high-heat setting for 2½ to 3 hours.

3 If using low-heat setting, turn to high-heat setting. Stir in tortellini. Cover and cook for 1 hour more.

Nutrition Facts per serving: 544 cal., 34 g total fat (16 g sat. fat), 114 mg chol., 2,247 mg sodium, 47 g carbo., 2 g fiber, 14 g pro.
Daily Values: 31% vit. A, 22% vit. C, 14% calcium, 11% iron

5

Appealing Appetizers and Beverages

Chicken Wings with Barbecue Sauce

Use your favorite barbecue sauce for this easy appetizer. Be sure to have plenty of napkins on hand to catch any drips!

Prep: 15 minutes Broil: 15 minutes Cook: Low 3 hours, High 1½ hours
Makes: about 32 appetizer servings

3 pounds chicken wings (about 16)
1½ cups bottled barbecue sauce
¼ cup honey
2 teaspoons prepared mustard
1½ teaspoons Worcestershire sauce

1 Use a sharp knife to carefully cut off tips of the wings; discard wing tips. Cut each wing at joint to make 2 pieces. Place wing pieces on the unheated rack of a broiler pan. Broil 4 to 5 inches from heat for 15 to 20 minutes or until chicken is browned, turning once.

2 For sauce, in a 3½- or 4-quart slow cooker combine barbecue sauce, honey, mustard, and Worcestershire sauce. Add wing pieces, stirring to coat with sauce.

3 Cover and cook on low-heat setting for 3 to 4 hours or on high-heat setting for 1½ to 2 hours.

Nutrition Facts per appetizer serving: 83 cal., 4 g total fat (1 g sat. fat), 20 mg chol., 197 mg sodium, 6 g carbo., 0 g fiber, 5 g pro.
Daily Values: 1% vit. A, 1% iron

Five-Spice Chicken Wings

Five-spice powder is a fragrant blend often used in Asian cooking. It usually includes cinnamon, anise seeds or star anise, fennel, black or Szechwan pepper, and cloves.

Prep: 20 minutes Bake: 20 minutes Cook: Low 4 hours, High 2 hours
Makes: about 16 appetizer servings

- 3 pounds chicken wings (about 16)
- 1 cup bottled plum sauce
- 2 tablespoons butter, melted
- 1 teaspoon five-spice powder
- Thin orange wedges and pineapple slices (optional)

1 Use a sharp knife to carefully cut off tips of the wings; discard wing tips. In a foil-lined 15×10×1-inch shallow baking pan arrange wings in a single layer. Bake in a 375°F oven for 20 minutes. Drain well.

2 For sauce, in a 3½- or 4-quart slow cooker combine plum sauce, melted butter, and five-spice powder. Add wings, stirring to coat with sauce.

3 Cover and cook on low-heat setting for 4 to 5 hours or on high-heat setting for 2 to 2½ hours. Serve immediately or keep warm on low-heat setting for up to 2 hours. If desired, garnish with orange wedges and pineapple slices.

Nutrition Facts per appetizer serving: 176 cal., 13 g total fat (3 g sat. fat), 70 mg chol., 82 mg sodium, 6 g carbo., 0 g fiber, 12 g pro. Daily Values: 1% vit. A, 2% calcium

Kentucky Chicken Wings: *Prepare chicken as in step 1. For sauce, in slow cooker combine ½ cup maple syrup, ½ cup whiskey, and 2 tablespoons melted butter. Add wings, stirring to coat with sauce. Continue as above in step 3.*

Cranberry-Sauced Franks

If you forget the cocktail wieners, you can cut frankfurters or cooked, smoked Polish sausage into 1½-inch pieces as a substitute.

Prep: 10 minutes Cook: Low 4 hours, High 2 hours Makes: 32 appetizer servings

- 1 cup bottled barbecue sauce
- 1 16-ounce can jellied cranberry sauce
- 2 1-pound packages cocktail wieners and/or small cooked smoked sausage links

1 For sauce, in a 3½- or 4-quart slow cooker stir together the barbecue sauce and cranberry sauce until combined. Add wieners and/or sausages, stirring to coat.

2 Cover and cook on low-heat setting for 4 to 5 hours or on high-heat setting for 2 to 2½ hours. Serve immediately or keep warm on low-heat setting for up to 2 hours. Serve with a slotted spoon or decorative toothpicks.

Nutrition Facts per appetizer serving: 118 cal., 8 g total fat (4 g sat. fat), 15 mg chol., 275 mg sodium, 8 g carbo., 0 g fiber, 3 g pro. Daily Values: 1% vit. A, 1% vit. C, 1% iron

Hot Honeyed Spareribs

These ribs are perfect for an open-house appetizer party because they stay warm in the honey-sweetened picante sauce.

Prep: 20 minutes Cook: Low 6 hours, High 3 hours Broil: 10 minutes
Makes: 10 to 12 appetizer servings

- 3½ to 4 pounds pork baby back ribs, cut into 1-rib portions
- 2 cups bottled picante sauce or salsa
- ½ cup honey
- 1 tablespoon quick-cooking tapioca
- 1 teaspoon ground ginger

1 Preheat broiler. Place ribs on the unheated rack of a broiler pan. Broil 6 inches from the heat about 10 minutes or until brown, turning once. Transfer ribs to a 3½- to 6-quart slow cooker.

2 For sauce, in a medium bowl combine picante sauce, honey, tapioca, and ginger. Pour sauce over ribs.

3 Cover and cook on low-heat setting for 6 to 7 hours or on high-heat setting for 3 to 3½ hours. Skim fat from sauce. Serve sauce with ribs.

Nutrition Facts per appetizer serving: 215 cal., 6 g total fat (2 g sat. fat), 43 mg chol., 246 mg sodium, 18 g carbo., 0 g fiber, 20 g pro.
Daily Values: 7% vit. C, 1% calcium, 4% iron

Plum Good Sausage and Meatballs

Although this recipe calls for a package of 16 meatballs, different brands contain different numbers of meatballs. You can substitute a package that contains 35 smaller meatballs.

Prep: 10 minutes Cook: Low 5 hours, High 2½ hours Makes: 16 appetizer servings

- 1 10- or 12-ounce jar plum jam or preserves
- 1 18-ounce bottle (1⅔ cups) barbecue sauce
- 1 16-ounce link cooked jalapeño smoked sausage or smoked sausage, sliced into bite-size pieces
- 1 16- to 18-ounce package Italian-style or original flavor frozen cooked meatballs (16), thawed

1 For sauce, in a 3½- or 4-quart slow cooker combine the jam and barbecue sauce. Add the sausage and thawed meatballs, stirring to coat with sauce.

2 Cover and cook on low-heat setting for 5 to 6 hours or on high-heat setting for 2½ to 3 hours. Serve immediately or keep warm on low-heat setting for up to 2 hours. Serve with decorative toothpicks.

Nutrition Facts per appetizer serving: 267 cal., 16 g total fat (6 g sat. fat), 38 mg chol., 898 mg sodium, 19 g carbo., 2 g fiber, 12 g pro. Daily Values: 6% vit. A, 7% vit. C, 3% calcium, 7% iron

Spicy Mustard Stir-Fry Bites

Wrapped and ready, these good-looking, bite-size fajitas are savory and filling.

Prep: 25 minutes Cook: Low 6 hours Makes: about 25 appetizer servings

Nonstick cooking spray
1 pound packaged chicken, pork, or beef stir-fry strips
½ cup water
½ cup spicy brown mustard
4 teaspoons fajita seasoning
5 7- to 8-inch flour tortillas, warmed*
1 medium red, green, and/or yellow sweet pepper, seeded and cut into thin strips
Snipped fresh cilantro and/or sliced green onion (optional)

1 Lightly coat a large skillet with cooking spray. Heat over medium-high heat; add stir-fry strips. Cook and stir until browned. Drain off fat.

2 For sauce, in a 1½-quart slow cooker combine water, mustard, and fajita seasoning. Add browned stir-fry strips, stirring to coat with sauce.

3 Cover and cook on low-heat setting, if available,** for 6 to 7 hours. Using a slotted spoon, remove meat from cooker. Use 2 forks to shred meat. Discard juices in the slow cooker.

4 Divide meat mixture evenly among the warmed tortillas. Top with sweet pepper strips and, if desired, cilantro and/or green onion. Roll up tortillas. Using a serrated knife, cut filled tortillas crosswise into bite-size pieces. If desired, skewer with decorative toothpicks.

***Note:** *To warm tortillas, stack tortillas and wrap tightly in foil. Heat in a 350°F oven about 10 minutes or until heated through.*

****Note:** *Some 1½-quart slow cookers include variable heat settings; others offer only one standard (low) setting. The 1½-quart slow cooker recipes in this book were only tested on the low-heat setting, if one was present.*

Nutrition Facts per appetizer serving: 47 cal., 1 g total fat (0 g sat. fat), 13 mg chol., 131 mg sodium, 4 g carbo., 0 g fiber, 5 g pro.
Daily Values: 7% vit. A, 19% vit. C, 2% calcium, 3% iron

Hoisin-Garlic Mushroom Appetizers

Cooked in hoisin sauce and spiced with garlic and red pepper flakes, bite-size button mushrooms pack a surprisingly large amount of flavor.

Prep: 15 minutes Cook: Low 5 hours, High 2½ hours Makes: 10 appetizer servings

- ½ cup bottled hoisin sauce
- ¼ cup water
- 2 tablespoons bottled minced garlic
- ¼ to ½ teaspoon crushed red pepper
- 24 ounces whole fresh button mushrooms, trimmed

1 For sauce, in a 3½- or 4-quart slow cooker combine hoisin sauce, water, garlic, and crushed red pepper. Add mushrooms, stirring to coat with sauce.

2 Cover and cook on low-heat setting for 5 to 6 hours or on high-heat setting for 2½ to 3 hours. To serve, remove mushrooms from cooker with a slotted spoon. Discard cooking liquid. Serve warm mushrooms with decorative toothpicks.

Nutrition Facts per appetizer serving: 39 cal., 1 g total fat (0 g sat. fat), 0 mg chol., 107 mg sodium, 6 g carbo., 1 g fiber, 3 g pro. Daily Values: 2% vit. C, 1% calcium, 3% iron

Sausage-Cheese Dip

Like things on the spicy side? Use chorizo in place of pork sausage.

Prep: 15 minutes Cook: Low 2 hours Makes: 24 (¼-cup) appetizer servings

1 pound bulk pork sausage
1 14½-ounce can diced tomatoes with garlic and onion, undrained
2 pounds process cheese product with jalapeño peppers, cubed
Toasted baguette slices or toasted pita wedges

1 In a large skillet cook meat over medium heat until no longer pink. Drain well. Transfer meat to a 3½- or 4-quart slow cooker. Stir in undrained tomatoes and cubed cheese.

2 Cover and cook on low-heat setting for 2 to 3 hours, stirring after 1 hour to mix in the cheese. Serve immediately or keep warm, covered, on low-heat setting for up to 2 hours, stirring occasionally. Serve with baguette slices or pita wedges.

Nutrition Facts per ¼ cup dip: 190 cal., 15 g total fat (9 g sat. fat), 37 mg chol., 671 mg sodium, 4 g carbo., 0 g fiber, 9 g pro.
Daily Values: 8% vit. A, 2% vit. C, 21% calcium, 2% iron

Sausage-Chili Dip

For a party, arrange a mass of various tortilla chips and fresh veggies around a bowl of this robust sauce.

Prep: 15 minutes Cook: Low 4 hours Makes: 24 (¼-cup) appetizer servings

- 8 ounces bulk Italian sausage
- 1 8-ounce package shredded American cheese (2 cups)
- 2 15-ounce cans chili without beans
- 1 cup bottled green salsa or salsa
- Assorted dippers, such as corn chips and/or red or green sweet pepper strips

1 In a medium skillet cook meat over medium heat until brown. Drain well. Transfer meat to a 3½- or 4-quart slow cooker. Stir in cheese, chili, and salsa.

2 Cover and cook on low-heat setting for 4 to 5 hours. Serve immediately or keep warm, covered, on low-heat setting for up to 2 hours, stirring occasionally. Stir just before serving with desired dippers.

Nutrition Facts per ¼ cup dip: 135 cal., 10 g total fat (5 g sat. fat), 24 mg chol., 398 mg sodium, 3 g carbo., 0 g fiber, 7 g pro.
Daily Values: 4% vit. A, 1% vit. C, 7% calcium, 4% iron

Cheesy Beer-Salsa Dip

To increase the kick for spice lovers at your party, use salsa that has plenty of heat.

Prep: 15 minutes Cook: Low 2 hours Makes: 22 (¼-cup) appetizer servings

- 1 16-ounce jar salsa
- 6 cups shredded American cheese (1½ pounds)
- 1 8-ounce package cream cheese, cut up
- ⅔ cup beer or milk
- Tortilla chips

1 In a 3½- or 4-quart slow cooker combine salsa, American cheese, cream cheese, and beer.

2 Cover and cook on low-heat setting for 2 to 3 hours. Serve immediately or keep warm, covered, on low-heat setting for up to 2 hours, stirring occasionally. Stir just before serving with tortilla chips.

Nutrition Facts per ¼ cup dip: 150 cal., 11 g total fat (7 g sat. fat), 31 mg chol., 543 mg sodium, 5 g carbo., 1 g fiber, 7 g pro.
Daily Values: 9% vit. A, 19% calcium, 2% iron

Chipotle Con Queso Dip

Tote this zesty appetizer to a tailgate party or dish it up while watching a game on television. Either way, just before serving, give it a good stir with a whisk to smooth it out.

Prep: 10 minutes Cook: Low 3 hours, High 1½ hours Makes: 16 (about ¼-cup) appetizer servings

- 2 pounds process cheese product, cubed
- 1 10-ounce can diced tomatoes and green chile peppers, undrained
- 1 to 3 chipotle peppers in adobo sauce, chopped
- 1 tablespoon Worcestershire sauce
- Tortilla chips

1 In a 3½- or 4-quart slow cooker combine the cubed cheese product, undrained tomatoes, chipotle peppers in adobo sauce, and Worcestershire sauce.

2 Cover and cook on low-heat setting for 3 to 3½ hours or on high-heat setting for 1½ to 1¾ hours. Serve immediately or keep warm, covered, on low-heat setting for up to 2 hours, stirring occasionally. Whisk before serving with tortilla chips.

Nutrition Facts per ¼ cup dip: 210 cal., 14 g total fat (9 g sat. fat), 47 mg chol., 880 mg sodium, 6 g carbo., 0 g fiber, 13 g pro.
Daily Values: 26% vit. A, 4% vit. C, 32% calcium, 1% iron

Creamy Avocado-Lime Dip

Lime juice gives this rich chip dip a citrusy twist. Spike it with hot pepper sauce, if you like, and scoop it up with a mix of plain and lime-flavored tortilla chips.

Prep: 15 minutes Cook: Low 2½ hours Stand: 15 minutes Makes: 16 (¼-cup) appetizer servings

- 2 limes
- 2 8-ounce tubs cream cheese with chive and onion
- 2 8-ounce cartons refrigerated guacamole dip
- ½ cup chopped onion (1 medium)
- Several dashes bottled hot pepper sauce (optional)
- Lime-flavored and/or plain tortilla chips

1 Finely shred the peel from the limes. Measure 1 teaspoon peel; set aside. Squeeze the juice from the limes. Measure 3 tablespoons juice; set aside.

2 In a 1½-quart slow cooker combine cream cheese, guacamole dip, onion, reserved lime peel and juice, and, if desired, hot pepper sauce.

3 Cover and cook on low-heat setting, if available,* for 2½ to 3 hours. Remove liner from cooker, if possible, or unplug cooker. Allow to stand 15 minutes before serving. Stir before serving with tortilla chips.

***Note:** *Some 1½-quart slow cookers include variable heat settings; others offer only one standard (low) setting. The 1½-quart slow cooker recipes in this book were only tested on the low-heat setting, if one was present.*

Nutrition Facts per ¼ cup dip: 156 cal., 13 g total fat (6 g sat. fat), 27 mg chol., 336 mg sodium, 5 g carbo., 0 g fiber, 2 g pro.
Daily Values: 7% vit. A, 2% vit. C, 4% calcium

Tomato Sauce with Garlic Cheese Bread

Leftover sauce? Serve it another night over your favorite hot cooked pasta for a quick meal.

Prep: 10 minutes Cook: Low 3 hours Makes: 14 (¼-cup) appetizer servings

- 1 14-ounce jar tomato pasta sauce (any flavor)
- 1 14½-ounce can diced tomatoes with basil, garlic, and oregano, undrained
- 1 2-ounce jar (drained weight) sliced mushrooms, drained
- ¼ cup finely shredded Parmesan cheese
- 1 11¾-ounce package frozen garlic cheese bread or garlic bread

1 In a 1½-quart slow cooker combine pasta sauce, undrained tomatoes, and drained mushrooms.

2 Cover and cook on low-heat setting, if available,* for 3 to 4 hours. Stir in Parmesan cheese.

3 Prepare garlic cheese bread according to package directions. Cut crosswise into slices. Serve sauce with cheese bread as dippers.

***Note:** *Some 1½-quart slow cookers include variable heat settings; others offer only one standard (low) setting. The 1½-quart slow cooker recipes in this book were only tested on the low-heat setting, if one was present.*

Nutrition Facts per appetizer serving with dippers: 90 cal., 3 g total fat (1 g sat. fat), 1 mg chol., 352 mg sodium, 10 g carbo., 1 g fiber, 4 g pro. Daily Values: 6% vit. A, 6% vit. C, 8% calcium, 4% iron

For a 3½-quart slow cooker: *In the cooker combine two 26-ounce jars pasta sauce; one 14½-ounce can diced tomatoes with basil, garlic, and oregano, undrained; and one 4- to 4½-ounce jar (drained weight) sliced mushrooms, drained. Cover and cook on low-heat setting for 6 to 8 hours or on high-heat setting for 3 to 4 hours. Stir in ½ cup Parmesan cheese. Prepare two 11¾-ounce packages frozen garlic cheese bread or garlic bread. Serve as above. Makes 26 (¼-cup) servings.*

Peanut Butter Cocoa

Kids will love this cocoa with a peanut buttery twist. After cooking is done, whisk in the creamy peanut butter (don't use chunky-style for this recipe).

Prep: 10 minutes Cook: Low 3 hours, High 1½ hours Makes: 9 (8-ounce) servings

- 1 cup instant milk chocolate or chocolate fudge cocoa mix
- 8 cups hot water
- ¾ cup chocolate-flavored syrup
- ¼ cup creamy peanut butter
- 1½ teaspoons vanilla

1 Place cocoa mix in a 3½- or 4-quart slow cooker. Carefully stir in hot water. Stir in chocolate-flavored syrup.

2 Cover and cook on low-heat setting for 3 to 4 hours or on high-heat setting for 1½ to 2 hours. Whisk in peanut butter and vanilla until smooth. Ladle into mugs.

Nutrition Facts per serving: 176 cal., 4 g total fat (1 g sat. fat), 1 mg chol., 115 mg sodium, 32 g carbo., 1 g fiber, 3 g pro.
Daily Values: 3% calcium, 2% iron

Three-Way Cocoa

Prepare a batch of this basic cocoa. If you like, add cinnamon before simmering or coffee crystals before serving. Offer marshmallows and whipped cream to spoon on top.

Prep: 10 minutes Cook: Low 3 hours, High 1½ hours Makes: 10 (6-ounce) servings

- ¾ cup sugar
- ½ cup unsweetened cocoa powder
- 8 cups milk
- 1 tablespoon vanilla
- Marshmallows or whipped cream (optional)

1 In a 3½- to 5-quart slow cooker combine sugar and cocoa powder. Stir in milk until combined.

2 Cover and cook on low-heat setting for 3 to 4 hours or on high-heat setting for 1½ to 2 hours.

3 Serve immediately or keep covered on low-heat setting for up to 2 hours. Just before serving, stir in vanilla. If desired, carefully beat milk mixture with a rotary beater until frothy. Ladle cocoa into mugs. If desired, top each serving with marshmallows or whipped cream.

Nutrition Facts per serving: 174 cal., 4 g total fat (2 g sat. fat), 15 mg chol., 98 mg sodium, 26 g carbo., 0 g fiber, 8 g pro.
Daily Values: 8% vit. A, 3% vit. C, 29% calcium, 4% iron

Spicy Cocoa: *Prepare as directed, except add 1 teaspoon ground cinnamon and ⅛ teaspoon ground nutmeg with the cocoa powder.*

Mocha Cocoa: *Prepare as directed, except add ¾ teaspoon instant coffee crystals to each mug of prepared cocoa; stir to mix.*

Honey-Mulled Apple Cider

Sweeten this warm drink with either honey or brown sugar. Cinnamon sticks make handy stirrers and add a bit of flavor.

Prep: 10 minutes Cook: Low 5 hours, High 2½ hours Makes: 10 (8-ounce) servings

6 inches stick cinnamon, broken
1 teaspoon whole allspice
1 teaspoon whole cloves
10 cups pasteurized apple cider or apple juice (2½ quarts)
⅓ cup honey or packed light brown sugar
Cinnamon sticks (optional)

1 For spice bag, cut a double thickness of 100-percent-cotton cheesecloth into a 6-inch square. Place broken stick cinnamon, allspice, and cloves in the center of the cloth. Bring the corners together and tie closed with clean kitchen string. In a 3½- to 5-quart slow cooker combine spice bag, apple cider, and honey.

2 Cover and cook on low-heat setting for 5 to 6 hours or on high-heat setting for 2½ to 3 hours.

3 Remove the spice bag and discard. Ladle into mugs. If desired, serve with cinnamon-stick stirrers.

Nutrition Facts per serving: 150 cal., 0 g total fat (0 g sat. fat), 0 mg chol., 8 mg sodium, 38 g carbo., 0 g fiber, 0 g pro.
Daily Values: 4% vit. C, 2% calcium, 5% iron

Spicy Cranberry Punch

Once the punch has simmered, set the slow cooker on low to keep the drinks at perfect sipping temperature down to the final serving. Set out cinnamon sticks to use as stirrers.

Prep: 10 minutes Cook: Low 4 hours, High 2 hours Makes: 18 (4-ounce) servings

8 inches stick cinnamon, broken
6 whole cloves
5 cups white grape juice
2⅔ cups water
1 12-ounce can frozen cranberry juice concentrate
Cinnamon sticks (optional)

1 For spice bag, cut a double thickness of 100-percent-cotton cheesecloth into a 6-inch square. Place broken stick cinnamon and cloves in the center of the cloth. Bring the corners together and tie closed with clean kitchen string. In a 3½- to 5-quart slow cooker combine spice bag, grape juice, water, and juice concentrate.

2 Cover and cook on low-heat setting for 4 to 6 hours or on high-heat setting for 2 to 2½ hours.

3 Remove the spice bag and discard. Serve immediately or keep warm on low-heat setting for up to 2 hours. Ladle punch into small mugs. If desired, serve with cinnamon-stick stirrers.

Nutrition Facts per serving: 44 cal., 0 g total fat (0 g sat. fat), 0 mg chol., 12 mg sodium, 11 g carbo., 0 g fiber, 0 g pro.
Daily Values: 17% vit. C

Hot Scarlet Wine Punch

For a special occasion, garnish each cup of this ruby-hued punch with a few cranberries threaded like beads onto cocktail skewers.

Prep: 5 minutes Cook: Low 3 hours, High 1½ hours; plus 30 minutes on High
Makes: 14 (4-ounce) servings

- 2 inches stick cinnamon
- 4 whole cloves
- 1 32-ounce bottle cranberry juice (4 cups)
- ⅓ cup packed brown sugar
- 1 750-milliliter bottle white Zinfandel or dry white wine
- Whole fresh cranberries (optional)

1 For spice bag, cut a double thickness of 100-percent-cotton cheesecloth into a 6-inch square. Place cinnamon and cloves in the center of the cloth. Bring the corners together and tie closed with clean kitchen string. In a 3½- or 4-quart slow cooker combine spice bag, cranberry juice, and brown sugar.

2 Cover and cook on low-heat setting for 3 to 4 hours or on high-heat setting for 1½ to 2 hours.

3 Remove the spice bag and discard. If using low-heat setting, turn to high-heat setting. Stir wine into punch. Cover and cook for 30 minutes more. Serve immediately or keep warm, covered, on low-heat setting for up to 2 hours. Ladle punch into small mugs. If desired, garnish with cranberries on skewers.

Nutrition Facts per serving: 99 cal., 0 g total fat (0 g sat. fat), 0 mg chol., 6 mg sodium, 16 g carbo., 0 g fiber, 0 g pro.
Daily Values: 43% vit. C, 1% calcium, 2% iron

Tomato Sipper

For a spicier sipper, add several drops of bottled hot pepper sauce. This is a perfect starter for a brunch or tailgate party. Garnish with celery sticks for a contrast in color.

Prep: 10 minutes Cook: Low 4 hours, High 2 hours Makes: 8 (6-ounce) servings

- 1 46-ounce can vegetable juice
- 1 stalk celery, halved crosswise
- 2 tablespoons packed brown sugar
- 2 tablespoons lemon juice
- 2 teaspoons Worcestershire sauce

1 In a 3½- or 4-quart slow cooker combine vegetable juice, celery stalk, brown sugar, lemon juice, and Worcestershire sauce.

2 Cover and cook on low-heat setting for 4 to 5 hours or on high-heat setting for 2 to 2½ hours. Discard celery halves. Ladle into mugs.

Nutrition Facts per serving: 50 cal., 0 g total fat (0 g sat. fat), 0 mg chol., 443 mg sodium, 11 g carbo., 1 g fiber, 1 g pro.
Daily Values: 27% vit. A, 71% vit. C, 3% calcium, 5% iron

6

Side Dishes from the Slow Cooker

Cranberry-Apple Spiced Beets

Beet lovers take note: Here's a luscious way to celebrate the harvest from your garden or farmer's market. The cranberry-apple drink is an unexpectedly good pairing with beets.

Prep: 25 minutes Cook: Low 6 hours, High 3 hours Makes: 8 to 10 servings

- 3 pounds medium beets, peeled and quartered
- ½ teaspoon apple pie spice
- 1 tablespoon quick-cooking tapioca
- 1 cup cranberry-apple drink
- 2 tablespoons butter or margarine (optional)

1 Place beets in a 3½- or 4-quart slow cooker. Sprinkle with apple pie spice and tapioca; pour cranberry-apple drink over all. If desired, dot with butter.

2 Cover and cook on low-heat setting for 6 to 7 hours or on high-heat setting for 3 to 3½ hours. To serve, remove beets from cooker; spoon some sauce over beets.

Nutrition Facts per serving: 75 cal., 0 g total fat (0 g sat. fat), 0 mg chol., 85 mg sodium, 17 g carbo., 3 g fiber, 2 g pro.
Daily Values: 1% vit. A, 22% vit. C, 2% calcium, 5% iron

Sweet Baby Carrots

Carrots and onions become irresistibly tender as they cook in a sauce of apple jelly and unassuming dillweed.

Prep: 10 minutes Cook: Low 6 hours, High 3 hours Stand: 2 minutes Makes: 8 to 10 servings

- 2 16-ounce packages peeled baby carrots
- 1 pound boiling onions (about 16), peeled, or one 16-ounce package frozen small whole onions
- ½ teaspoon dried dillweed
- ¾ cup water
- 1 cup apple jelly

1 In a 4½- to 5½-quart slow cooker combine carrots and onions. Sprinkle with dillweed. Pour water over all.

2 Cover and cook on low-heat setting for 6 to 7 hours or on high-heat setting for 3 to 3½ hours.

3 Using a slotted spoon, remove carrots and onions from cooker. Gently stir in apple jelly; let stand for 2 to 3 minutes or until jelly is melted. Stir sauce. Return carrots and onions to sauce in cooker. Stir gently to coat vegetables. Serve with a slotted spoon.

Nutrition Facts per serving: 178 cal., 0 g total fat (0 g sat. fat), 0 mg chol., 53 mg sodium, 43 g carbo., 5 g fiber, 2 g pro.
Daily Values: 574% vit. A, 19% vit. C, 5% calcium, 4% iron

Cheesy Cauliflower for a Crowd

This side dish, made super convenient with a jar of cheese pasta sauce, is perfect for your next potluck.

Prep: 15 minutes Cook: Low 6 hours, High 3 hours Makes: 10 to 12 servings

- 8 cups cauliflower florets
- 1 large onion, thinly sliced
- ½ teaspoon fennel seeds, crushed
- 1 14- to 16-ounce jar cheddar cheese pasta sauce
- Cracked black pepper

1 In a 3½- or 4-quart slow cooker place cauliflower, onion, and fennel seeds. Pour pasta sauce over all.

2 Cover and cook on low-heat setting for 6 to 7 hours or on high-heat setting for 3 to 3½ hours. Stir gently. Sprinkle with pepper before serving.

Nutrition Facts per serving: 59 cal., 6 g total fat (2 g sat. fat), 16 mg chol., 329 mg sodium, 8 g carbo., 2 g fiber, 3 g pro.
Daily Values: 3% vit. A, 54% vit. C, 7% calcium, 3% iron

Creamy Corn and Roasted Red Peppers

A creamy consistency, pleasing tang, and pretty hue make this dish a welcome contribution to any buffet.

Prep: 15 minutes Cook: Low 6 hours, High 3 hours Makes: 8 servings

3 10-ounce packages frozen whole kernel corn or white whole kernel corn (shoe peg) in light or regular butter sauce
1 12-ounce jar roasted red sweet peppers, drained and chopped (about 1 cup)
2 tablespoons thinly sliced green onion (1)
2 cups milk
2 0.88- to 1.5-ounce envelopes hollandaise sauce mix

1 In a 3½-quart slow cooker place frozen corn, sweet peppers, and green onion. In a small mixing bowl whisk together milk and sauce mix. Add sauce mixture to cooker; stir to combine (frozen chunks of vegetables may remain).

2 Cover and cook on low-heat setting for 6 to 8 hours or on high-heat setting for 3 to 4 hours. Stir before serving.

Nutrition Facts per serving: 155 cal., 2 g total fat (1 g sat. fat), 5 mg chol., 249 mg sodium, 32 g carbo., 2 g fiber, 5 g pro.
Daily Values: 3% vit. A, 98% vit. C, 8% calcium, 4% iron

Cheesy Succotash

Corn and lima beans join onions in a thick cream cheese-based sauce.

Prep: 15 minutes Cook: Low 7 hours, High 3½ hours Makes: 12 servings

- 2 16-ounce packages frozen whole kernel corn
- 1 16-ounce package frozen lima beans
- 1 cup frozen small whole onions
- 1 10¾-ounce can condensed cream of celery soup
- 1 8-ounce tub cream cheese with chive and onion
- ¼ cup water

1 In a 4- or 4½-quart slow cooker combine frozen corn, lima beans, and onions. In a medium bowl stir together soup, cream cheese, and water. Stir soup mixture into vegetables in cooker.

2 Cover and cook on low-heat setting for 7 to 8 hours or on high-heat setting for 3½ to 4 hours. Stir before serving.

Nutrition Facts per serving: 211 cal., 8 g total fat (5 g sat. fat), 19 mg chol., 296 mg sodium, 29 g carbo., 4 g fiber, 6 g pro.
Daily Values: 8% vit. A, 15% vit. C, 5% calcium, 7% iron

Swiss Potatoes and Asparagus

Creamy, thick, and rich, this is the kind of asparagus dish you expect to find at an elegant brunch. Serve it with hot scrambled eggs and sliced fresh fruit.

Prep: 15 minutes Cook: Low 5 hours; plus 15 minutes on Low Makes: 10 to 12 servings

Nonstick cooking spray
1 10¾-ounce can condensed cream of asparagus soup
8 ounces process Swiss cheese, cut into ½-inch pieces
1 8-ounce carton dairy sour cream
1 32-ounce package frozen loose-pack diced hash brown potatoes, thawed
1 10-ounce package frozen cut asparagus, thawed

1 Lightly coat a 3½- or 4-quart slow cooker with cooking spray. In the prepared cooker stir together soup, cheese, and sour cream. Stir in potatoes.

2 Cover and cook on low-heat setting for 5 to 6 hours. Stir in asparagus. Cover and cook for 15 to 25 minutes more or until heated through.

Nutrition Facts per serving: 237 cal., 12 g total fat (7 g sat. fat), 32 mg chol., 311 mg sodium, 22 g carbo., 2 g fiber, 11 g pro.
Daily Values: 13% vit. A, 29% vit. C, 27% calcium, 7% iron

Creamy Potato Wedges

Looking for please-all postgame party fare? This dish is a favorite appetizer: slow cooking transforms it into a scoopable side dish.

Prep: 10 minutes Cook: Low 3½ hours, High 1¾ hours Makes: 8 servings

- 2 8-ounce containers dairy sour cream chive dip
- 1 cup finely shredded Asiago cheese (4 ounces)
- 1 3-ounce package cream cheese, cut up
- ½ cup mayonnaise
- 2 20-ounce packages refrigerated new potato wedges

1 In a 3½- or 4-quart slow cooker combine sour cream dip, Asiago cheese, cream cheese, and mayonnaise. Stir in refrigerated potatoes.

2 Cover and cook on low-heat setting for 3½ to 4½ hours or on high-heat setting for 1¾ to 2¼ hours. Stir gently before serving.

Nutrition Facts per serving: 415 cal., 31 g total fat (14 g sat. fat), 55 mg chol., 835 mg sodium, 23 g carbo., 4 g fiber, 10 g pro.
Daily Values: 11% vit. A, 8% vit. C, 20% calcium, 5% iron

Saucy Green Beans and Potatoes

Tender potatoes and crisp green beans achieve elegance in a mustard-dill sauce that's just right accompanying Sunday dinner's roast, beef tenderloin, or salmon.

Prep: 20 minutes Cook: Low 6 hours, High 3 hours Makes: 12 servings

- 2 pounds tiny new potatoes
- 1 pound fresh green beans, trimmed and halved crosswise
- 1 10¾-ounce can condensed cream of celery soup
- ¾ cup water
- ¼ cup Dijon-style mustard
- ¾ teaspoon dried dillweed

1 In a 3½- or 4-quart slow cooker combine potatoes and green beans. In a medium bowl stir together soup, water, mustard, and dillweed. Pour over vegetables in cooker; stir gently to combine.

2 Cover and cook on low-heat setting for 6 to 8 hours or on high-heat setting for 3 to 4 hours. Stir gently before serving.

Nutrition Facts per serving: 95 cal., 2 g total fat (1 g sat. fat), 1 mg chol., 313 mg sodium, 17 g carbo., 3 g fiber, 3 g pro.
Daily Values: 6% vit. A, 26% vit. C, 3% calcium, 8% iron

Super Creamy Mashed Potatoes

When you make a decadent dish like this, it's best to serve it at a gathering so you won't be tempted to indulge in the luscious leftovers.

Prep: 10 minutes Cook: Low 3½ hours Makes: 12 to 14 servings

Nonstick cooking spray
3 20-ounce packages refrigerated mashed potatoes or 8 cups leftover mashed potatoes
1 8-ounce package cream cheese, cut up
1 8-ounce container dairy sour cream onion or chive dip
¼ teaspoon garlic powder

1 Coat a 4- or 4½-quart slow cooker with cooking spray. Place 2 packages of the potatoes in the prepared cooker. Top with cut-up cream cheese and sour cream dip. Sprinkle with garlic powder. Top with remaining mashed potatoes.

2 Cover and cook on low-heat setting for 3½ to 4 hours. Stir before serving.

Nutrition Facts per serving: 214 cal., 11 g total fat (6 g sat. fat), 21 mg chol., 409 mg sodium, 22 g carbo., 1 g fiber, 5 g pro. Daily Values: 5% vit. A, 40% vit. C, 3% calcium, 5% iron

Hash Browns with Garlic-Mushroom Sauce

Plain hash browns show some personality when cooked with mushrooms, Swiss cheese, and garlic. You'll like this with eggs or meat, even straight from the pot.

Prep: 15 minutes Cook: Low 8 hours, High 4 hours Makes: 8 to 10 servings

1 32-ounce package frozen loose-pack diced hash brown potatoes
2 cups shredded Swiss cheese (8 ounces)
2 4-ounce cans sliced mushrooms, drained
1 tablespoon bottled roasted minced garlic
1 10¾-ounce can condensed cream of mushroom soup
¼ cup water

1 In a 3½- or 4-quart slow cooker combine frozen potatoes, cheese, mushrooms, and garlic. Add soup and water; stir to combine.

2 Cover and cook on low-heat setting for 8 to 9 hours or on high-heat setting for 4 to 4½ hours. Stir gently before serving.

Nutrition Facts per serving: 248 cal., 11 g total fat (6 g sat. fat), 26 mg chol., 482 mg sodium, 26 g carbo., 3 g fiber, 12 g pro.
Daily Values: 5% vit. A, 18% vit. C, 30% calcium, 9% iron

Creamy Ranch Potatoes

These rich and creamy potatoes are so easy and delicious that leftovers are unheard of.

Prep: 15 minutes Cook: Low 7 hours, High 3½ hours Makes: 6 servings

- 2½ pounds small red potatoes, quartered
- 1 10¾-ounce can condensed cream of mushroom soup
- 1 8-ounce carton dairy sour cream
- 1 0.4-ounce envelope buttermilk ranch dry salad dressing mix

1 Place potatoes in a 3½- or 4-quart slow cooker. In a small bowl stir together soup, sour cream, and salad dressing mix. Stir soup mixture into potatoes to combine.

2 Cover and cook on low-heat setting for 7 to 8 hours or on high-heat setting for 3½ to 4 hours. Stir gently before serving.

Nutrition Facts per serving: 245 cal., 12 g total fat (6 g sat. fat), 17 mg chol., 517 mg sodium, 30 g carbo., 2 g fiber, 5 g pro.
Daily Values: 6% vit. A, 31% vit. C, 7% calcium, 12% iron

Apple-Buttered Sweet Potatoes

This side dish is so delectable, it could double for dessert. Dried fruit adds a tart dimension.

Prep: 15 minutes Cook: Low 6 hours, High 3 hours Makes: 10 servings

- 3 pounds sweet potatoes, peeled and cut into 1-inch pieces
- 2 medium Granny Smith or other tart cooking apples, peeled, cored, and cut into wedges
- ½ cup dried cherries or dried cranberries (optional)
- 1 cup whipping cream
- 1 cup apple butter
- 1½ teaspoons pumpkin pie spice

1 In a 3½- or 4-quart slow cooker combine sweet potatoes, apples, and, if desired, cherries. In a medium bowl combine whipping cream, apple butter, and pumpkin pie spice. Gently stir apple butter mixture into sweet potato mixture to combine.

2 Cover and cook on low-heat setting for 6 to 7 hours or on high-heat setting for 3 to 3½ hours.

Nutrition Facts per serving: 351 cal., 9 g total fat (6 g sat. fat), 33 mg chol., 25 mg sodium, 65 g carbo., 5 g fiber, 2 g pro.
Daily Values: 363% vit. A, 28% vit. C, 5% calcium, 5% iron

Winter Squash in Cherry Sauce

Tender cubed squash infused with onion and thyme and immersed in cherry sauce renders a sweet and savory surprise. Its rich orange-red color scores a festive point.

Prep: 20 minutes Cook: Low 8 hours, High 4 hours Makes: 6 to 8 servings

- 1 21-ounce can cherry pie filling
- 2 pounds butternut or other winter squash, peeled, seeded, and cut into ¾-inch pieces (about 4½ cups)
- 1 medium onion, cut into wedges
- ½ teaspoon dried thyme, crushed
- ½ cup chopped pecans, toasted*

1 In a 3½- or 4-quart slow cooker combine pie filling, squash, onion, and thyme.

2 Cover and cook on low-heat setting for 8 to 9 hours or on high-heat setting for 4 to 4½ hours. Cool slightly before serving. Sprinkle each serving with pecans.

***Note:** *To toast nuts, spread nuts in a single layer in a shallow baking pan. Bake in a 350°F oven for 5 to 10 minutes or until light golden brown, watching carefully and stirring once or twice so the nuts don't burn.*

Nutrition Facts per serving: 223 cal., 7 g total fat (1 g sat. fat), 0 mg chol., 23 mg sodium, 40 g carbo., 3 g fiber, 3 g pro.
Daily Values: 88% vit. A, 26% vit. C, 5% calcium, 7% iron

Western Beans

Hot-style barbecue sauce and dry mustard step in for bacon, and a new kind of vegetarian baked bean arrives—with just a bit of heat.

Prep: 15 minutes Cook: Low 4 hours, High 2 hours Makes: 12 servings

- 3 28-ounce cans vegetarian baked beans, drained
- ¾ cup bottled hot-style barbecue sauce
- ½ cup chopped onion (1 medium)
- ⅓ cup packed brown sugar
- 1 tablespoon dry mustard

1 In a 3½- to 5-quart slow cooker combine beans, barbecue sauce, onion, brown sugar, and mustard.

2 Cover and cook on low-heat setting for 4 to 5 hours or on high-heat setting for 2 to 2½ hours.

Nutrition Facts per serving: 238 cal., 1 g total fat (0 g sat. fat), 0 mg chol., 1,015 mg sodium, 53 g carbo., 10 g fiber, 10 g pro.
Daily Values: 8% vit. A, 13% vit. C, 11% calcium, 5% iron

Apricot-Bacon Beans

An intriguing variation of classic baked beans, this version gets a hint of saucy sweetness by way of apricot preserves. Show it off at your next picnic; it's great with grilled burgers.

Prep: 15 minutes Cook: Low 8 hours, High 4 hours Makes: 12 to 16 servings

- 2 28-ounce cans beans with brown sugar or baked beans, or four 15- to 16-ounce cans Great Northern, lima, and/or pinto beans
- 1 10- to 12-ounce jar apricot preserves
- 1 cup chopped celery
- ½ cup packed brown sugar
- 8 slices peppered bacon, crisp-cooked, drained, and crumbled

1. If using beans with brown sugar or baked beans, do not rinse or drain. If using Great Northern, lima, or pinto beans, rinse and drain beans.

2. In a 3½- or 4-quart slow cooker combine beans, preserves, celery, brown sugar, and bacon.

3. Cover and cook on low-heat setting for 8 to 10 hours or on high-heat setting for 4 to 5 hours.

Nutrition Facts per serving: 343 cal., 9 g total fat (4 g sat. fat), 19 mg chol., 631 mg sodium, 53 g carbo., 7 g fiber, 9 g pro.
Daily Values: 3% vit. A, 11% vit. C, 10% calcium, 15% iron

Triple-Cheesy Pasta Sauce

Soup, Alfredo sauce, and Parmesan cheese combine for a thick and saucy triple treat. Spoon the sauce over cheese tortellini or your favorite kind of pasta.

Prep: 10 minutes Cook: Low 4 hours, High 2 hours Makes: 12 servings

- 2 10¾-ounce cans condensed broccoli cheese or cheddar cheese soup
- 1 16-ounce jar Alfredo pasta sauce
- ¼ cup grated Parmesan cheese (1 ounce)
- 1 teaspoon garlic-pepper seasoning
- 2 cups water
- 3 9-ounce packages refrigerated cheese-filled tortellini or 1 pound dried pasta (any shape)

1 In a 3½- or 4-quart slow cooker combine soup, Alfredo pasta sauce, Parmesan cheese, and garlic-pepper seasoning. Stir in water.

2 Cover and cook on low-heat setting for 4 to 5 hours or on high-heat setting for 2 to 2½ hours.

3 Prepare tortellini according to package directions; drain. Stir cooked pasta into sauce. Serve immediately.

Nutrition Facts per serving: 317 cal., 14 g total fat (7 g sat. fat), 61 mg chol., 976 mg sodium, 35 g carbo., 3 g fiber, 13 g pro.
Daily Values: 16% vit. A, 1% vit. C, 18% calcium, 8% iron

Ginger Pea Pods and Noodles

Snow pea pods are spicy and piquant cooked in a gingery stir-fry sauce with angel hair or spaghettini pasta. When your main dish is simple, let this side provide the excitement.

Prep: 15 minutes Cook: Low 5 hours, High 2½ hours; plus 15 minutes on High Makes: 8 servings

- 2 14-ounce cans chicken or vegetable broth (3½ cups)
- 1 cup bottled stir-fry sauce
- 1 tablespoon bottled grated ginger
- 4 cups fresh snow pea pods (8 ounces)
- 12 ounces dried angel hair or spaghettini pasta, broken

1 In a 3½- or 4-quart slow cooker stir together broth, stir-fry sauce, and ginger. Add pea pods; stir gently to mix.

2 Cover and cook on low-heat setting for 5 to 6 hours or on high-heat setting for 2½ to 3 hours.

3 If using low-heat setting, turn to high-heat setting. Stir in uncooked pasta. Gently press pasta with a spoon to cover with the liquid. Cover and cook for 15 to 20 minutes more or until pasta is tender.

Nutrition Facts per serving: 225 cal., 2 g total fat (0 g sat. fat), 0 mg chol., 1,482 mg sodium, 43 g carbo., 2 g fiber, 8 g pro.
Daily Values: 3% vit. A, 29% vit. C, 4% calcium, 15% iron

Saucy Sweet Pepper Pasta

Red, orange, yellow, and green sweet peppers brighten cheese ravioli. This makes a fine accompaniment to salmon or tuna, whether grilled or broiled.

Prep: 20 minutes Cook: Low 6 hours, High 3 hours; plus 30 minutes on High
Makes: 10 to 12 servings

- 4 medium red, green, orange, and/or yellow sweet peppers, cut into bite-size strips (about 4 cups)
- 2 14½-ounce cans diced tomatoes with basil, garlic, and oregano, undrained
- 1 15-ounce can tomato sauce
- ¼ to ½ teaspoon crushed red pepper
- 1 9-ounce package refrigerated cheese-filled tortellini

1 In a 3½- or 4-quart slow cooker combine sweet pepper strips, undrained tomatoes, tomato sauce, and crushed red pepper.

2 Cover and cook on low-heat setting for 6 to 8 hours or on high-heat setting for 3 to 4 hours. If using low-heat setting, turn to high-heat setting. Stir in tortellini. Cover and cook about 30 minutes more or until tortellini is tender.

Nutrition Facts per serving: 134 cal., 2 g total fat (1 g sat. fat), 12 mg chol., 713 mg sodium, 24 g carbo., 2 g fiber, 6 g pro.
Daily Values: 61% vit. A, 138% vit. C, 10% calcium, 12% iron

Wild Rice Pilaf with Squash

A nice match whether you're serving fish, chicken, or beef, winter squash and oranges boost the nutrients in this pilaf.

Prep: 20 minutes Cook: Low 4 hours, High 2 hours Makes: 8 to 10 servings

- 2 large oranges
- 3 cups peeled, seeded winter squash cut into bite-size pieces (such as butternut)
- 2 4.1- to 4.5-ounce packages long grain and wild rice mix with herbs (not quick-cooking)
- ¼ cup packed brown sugar
- 2 14-ounce cans chicken broth (3½ cups)

1 Finely shred the peel from one of the oranges. Measure 1 teaspoon finely shredded orange peel; set aside. Squeeze juice from both oranges. Measure ⅔ cup orange juice; set aside.

2 In a 3½- or 4-quart slow cooker combine squash, rice mixes and the contents of both rice seasoning packets, and the brown sugar. Add orange peel and orange juice. Pour chicken broth over all. Stir to combine.

3 Cover and cook on low-heat setting for 4 to 5 hours or on high-heat setting for 2 to 3 hours. Stir gently before serving.

Nutrition Facts per serving: 170 cal., 1 g total fat (0 g sat. fat), 0 mg chol., 931 mg sodium, 37 g carbo., 1 g fiber, 4 g pro.
Daily Values: 81% vit. A, 33% vit. C, 5% calcium, 8% iron

Sausage and Corn Bread Stuffing

This stuffing dons a Southern flair. If you're serving a crowd at a big holiday feast, set out both this version and the Raisin-Herb Seasoned Stuffing *(see recipe, page 206).*

Prep: 20 minutes Cook: Low 4 hours Makes: 10 to 12 servings

Nonstick cooking spray
1 pound bulk pork sausage
1 cup chopped onion (1 large)
1 16-ounce package corn bread stuffing mix
3 cups chicken broth
½ cup butter or margarine, melted

1 Lightly coat a 3½- to 4½-quart slow cooker with cooking spray; set aside.

2 In a large skillet cook meat and onion until meat is brown and onion is tender. Drain off fat. In the prepared cooker combine the stuffing mix, meat mixture, broth, and butter. Toss gently to mix well.

3 Cover and cook on low-heat setting for 4 to 5 hours.

Nutrition Facts per serving: 466 cal., 30 g total fat (13 g sat. fat), 57 mg chol., 1,214 mg sodium, 37 g carbo., 0 g fiber, 11 g pro.
Daily Values: 7% vit. A, 3% vit. C, 2% calcium, 11% iron

Raisin-Herb Seasoned Stuffing

It's holiday time and your oven is full. Put a slow cooker on stuffing duty. This savory herb-onion version gets a sweet note from raisins.

Prep: 20 minutes Cook: Low 5 hours, High 2½ hours Makes: 8 to 10 servings

- Nonstick cooking spray
- 1 16-ounce package herb-seasoned stuffing mix
- 1 cup golden and/or dark raisins
- ½ cup chopped onion (1 medium)
- 1½ cups water
- 1 10¾-ounce can condensed golden mushroom soup
- 1 8-ounce carton dairy sour cream

1 Lightly coat a 3½- or 4-quart slow cooker with cooking spray. In the prepared cooker combine stuffing mix, raisins, and onion. In a medium bowl combine water, soup, and sour cream. Pour soup mixture over stuffing mixture in cooker; stir gently to combine.

2 Cover and cook on low-heat setting for 5 to 6 hours or on high-heat setting for 2½ to 3 hours.

Nutrition Facts per serving: 377 cal., 9 g total fat (4 g sat. fat), 14 mg chol., 1,105 mg sodium, 65 g carbo., 6 g fiber, 9 g pro.
Daily Values: 9% vit. A, 2% vit. C, 10% calcium, 16% iron

7

Tempting Desserts

Chocolate-Caramel Fondue

It's important to swirl this decadent dessert as you dip to keep the chocolate mixture from setting up.

Prep: 10 minutes Cook: Low 2 hours Makes: 12 servings (3¼ cups)

1 14-ounce can (1¼ cups) sweetened condensed milk
1 12- to 12½-ounce container caramel ice cream topping
9 ounces semisweet chocolate, coarsely chopped, or 1½ cups semisweet chocolate pieces
Assorted dippers, such as angel food or pound cake cubes, large marshmallows, dried apricots, or fresh fruit including strawberries, banana slices, and/or pineapple chunks
Milk

1 In a 1½-quart slow cooker stir together sweetened condensed milk, ice cream topping, and chocolate.

2 Cover and cook on low-heat setting, if available,* for 2 hours. Stir until mixture is smooth. Serve immediately or keep warm, covered, on low-heat setting for up to 1 hour (chocolate mixture will become grainy if held longer).

3 To serve, spear dippers with fondue forks. Dip into chocolate mixture, swirling as you dip. If the mixture thickens, stir in a little warm milk to make fondue of desired consistency.

*__Note:__ *Some 1½-quart slow cookers include variable heat settings; others offer only one standard (low) setting. The 1½-quart slow cooker recipes in this book were only tested on the low-heat setting, if one was present.*

Nutrition Facts per serving (fondue only): 295 cal., 10 g total fat (6 g sat. fat), 11 mg chol., 104 mg sodium, 50 g carbo., 2 g fiber, 6 g pro. Daily Values: 2% vit. A, 1% vit. C, 14% calcium, 6% iron

Slow-Cooked Apple Betty

Celebrate autumn with a visit to your local orchard and turn your finds into an apple betty. Tart apples and apple butter cook with brown sugar and cinnamon-raisin bread.

Prep: 25 minutes Cook: Low 4 hours Stand: 30 minutes Makes: 6 to 8 servings

- Nonstick cooking spray
- 5 tart cooking apples, peeled, cored, and sliced (5 cups)
- ¾ cup packed brown sugar
- ⅔ cup apple butter
- ½ cup water
- 5 cups soft cinnamon-raisin bread cut into ½-inch cubes (about 5 slices)
- ⅓ cup butter, melted
- Caramel ice cream topping and/or vanilla ice cream (optional)

1 Lightly coat a 3½- or 4-quart slow cooker with cooking spray; set aside.

2 In a medium bowl combine the apples, brown sugar, apple butter, and water. Toss until coated. In a medium bowl place the bread cubes. Drizzle with the melted butter, tossing until mixed.

3 Place half of the buttered bread cubes in prepared cooker. Pour all of the apple mixture over bread cubes. Sprinkle remaining bread cubes over apple mixture.

4 Cover and cook on low-heat setting about 4 hours. Remove liner from cooker, if possible, or turn off cooker. Let stand, uncovered, about 30 minutes to cool slightly before serving.

5 To serve, spoon warm dessert into dessert dishes. If desired, top with caramel ice cream topping and/or a scoop of vanilla ice cream.

Nutrition Facts per serving: 492 cal., 12 g total fat (7 g sat. fat), 29 mg chol., 209 mg sodium, 97 g carbo., 5 g fiber, 2 g pro.
Daily Values: 11% vit. A, 9% vit. C, 6% calcium, 8% iron

Tropical Apricot Crisp

The toasted coconut takes your palate to warmer climates. Dried tropical fruit bits combine with apricot pie filling for intense flavor.

Prep: 10 minutes Cook: Low 2½ hours Stand: 30 minutes Makes: 6 servings

Nonstick cooking spray
2 21-ounce cans apricot pie filling
1 7-ounce package tropical blend mixed dried fruit bits
1 cup granola
⅓ cup toasted coconut
1 pint vanilla ice cream

1 Lightly coat a 3½- or 4-quart slow cooker with cooking spray. In the prepared cooker combine the pie filling and dried fruit bits.

2 Cover and cook on low-heat setting for 2½ hours. Remove liner from cooker, if possible, or turn off cooker. In a small bowl combine granola and coconut. Sprinkle over fruit mixture in cooker. Let stand, uncovered, for 30 minutes to cool slightly before serving.

3 To serve, spoon warm mixture into dessert dishes. Top with a small scoop of vanilla ice cream.

Nutrition Facts per serving: 587 cal., 13 g total fat (8 g sat. fat), 45 mg chol., 144 mg sodium, 109 g carbo., 7 g fiber, 6 g pro.
Daily Values: 11% vit. A, 46% vit. C, 18% calcium, 9% iron

Peach and Tropical Fruit Cobbler

For a taste of sunshine any time of year, slow cook peach pie filling, tropical fruit salad, and cinnamon snack cake mix. The finished cobbler is mellow and moist.

Prep: 10 minutes Cook: High 2½ hours Stand: 45 minutes Makes: 10 servings

- Nonstick cooking spray
- 2 21-ounce cans peach pie filling (more fruit)
- 1 15¼-ounce can tropical fruit salad, undrained
- 1 13.9-ounce package cinnamon swirl snack cake mix
- ½ cup chopped pecans, toasted*
- 4½ cups vanilla ice cream

1 Lightly coat a 3½- or 4-quart slow cooker with cooking spray. In the prepared cooker combine the pie filling and undrained fruit salad.

2 Cover and cook on high-heat setting for 1½ hours or until fruit mixture is hot and bubbly; stir fruit mixture.

3 Prepare snack cake mix according to package directions; stir in pecans. Spoon cake batter over fruit mixture. Cover and cook on high-heat setting 1 hour more or until a wooden toothpick inserted near center of cake comes out clean. Remove liner from cooker, if possible, or turn off cooker. Let stand, uncovered, for 45 to 60 minutes to cool slightly before serving.

4 To serve, spoon warm cobbler into dessert dishes. Top with a scoop of ice cream.

***Note:** *To toast nuts, spread nuts in a single layer in a shallow baking pan. Bake in a 350°F oven for 5 to 10 minutes or until light golden brown, watching carefully and stirring once or twice so the nuts don't burn.*

Nutrition Facts per serving: 497 cal., 19 g total fat (8 g sat. fat), 61 mg chol., 309 mg sodium, 77 g carbo., 2 g fiber, 6 g pro.
Daily Values: 9% vit. A, 26% vit. C, 12% calcium, 6% iron

Pineapple-Peach Cobbler

Have the kids help you make this one. Mellow cooked fruit becomes a cobbler beneath fluffy iced cinnamon rolls.

Prep: 15 minutes Cook: High 1½ hours; plus 1 hour on High Stand: 30 minutes Makes: 8 servings

Nonstick cooking spray
2 21-ounce cans pineapple pie filling
1 6- or 7-ounce package dried peaches, snipped
½ cup orange juice
1 17½-ounce package (5) refrigerated large cinnamon rolls
Vanilla ice cream (optional)

1 Lightly coat a 3½- or 4-quart slow cooker with cooking spray. In the prepared cooker combine the pie filling, dried peaches, and orange juice.

2 Cover and cook on high-heat setting for 1½ hours or until fruit mixture is hot and bubbly; stir fruit mixture. Place cinnamon rolls on a cutting board, cinnamon side up (set icing aside). Cut each roll in half to make 2 semicircles. Place rolls on top of fruit mixture in cooker, cinnamon side up.

3 Cover and cook on high-heat setting 1 hour more or until rolls are fluffy all the way through. Remove liner from cooker, if possible, or turn off cooker. Let the cobbler stand, uncovered, for 30 to 45 minutes to cool slightly before serving. Spread icing over rolls.

4 To serve, spoon warm cobbler into dessert dishes. If desired, top with a scoop of vanilla ice cream.

Nutrition Facts per serving: 467 cal., 8 g total fat (2 g sat. fat), 0 mg chol., 493 mg sodium, 96 g carbo., 2 g fiber, 4 g pro.
Daily Values: 7% vit. A, 17% vit. C, 3% calcium, 22% iron

Mixed Berry Cobbler

With its intense berry flavor and muffinlike cake, cobbler wins a place on the list of classic summer fare. This method lets you enjoy it without heating up the kitchen.

Prep: 15 minutes Cook: Low 3 hours; plus 1 hour on High Stand: 30 minutes
Makes: 8 to 10 servings

Nonstick cooking spray
1 14-ounce package frozen loose-pack mixed berries
1 21-ounce can blueberry pie filling
¼ cup sugar
1 6½-ounce package blueberry or triple-berry muffin mix
⅓ cup water
2 tablespoons cooking oil
Vanilla ice cream (optional)

1 Lightly coat a 3½- or 4-quart slow cooker with cooking spray; set aside.

2 In a bowl combine frozen mixed berries, blueberry pie filling, and sugar. Place berry mixture in the bottom of the prepared cooker.

3 Cover and cook on low-heat setting for 3 hours. Turn cooker to high-heat setting. In a medium bowl combine muffin mix, water, and oil; stir just until combined. Spoon muffin mixture over berry mixture. Cover and cook for 1 hour more or until a wooden toothpick inserted into center of muffin mixture comes out clean. Remove liner from cooker, if possible, or turn off cooker. Let stand, uncovered, for 30 to 45 minutes to cool slightly before serving.

4 To serve, spoon warm cobbler into dessert dishes. If desired, top with a scoop of vanilla ice cream.

Nutrition Facts per serving: 250 cal., 6 g total fat (1 g sat. fat), 0 mg chol., 182 mg sodium, 48 g carbo., 5 g fiber, 1 g pro.
Daily Values: 1% calcium, 6% iron

Fruity Rice Pudding

Soft and comforting rice pudding dotted with bold bits of dried fruit lies under a bed of toasted nuts—a lovely dessert to follow grilled steak or salmon.

Prep: 15 minutes Cook: Low 2 hours Stand: 30 minutes Makes: 8 servings

- Nonstick cooking spray
- 2 5½-ounce packages rice pudding mix with raisins and spice
- 3 cups whole milk
- ½ cup snipped dried apricots or snipped dried cherries
- 2 tablespoons butter or margarine, softened
- ⅓ cup pecans or almonds, toasted*

1 Lightly coat a 3½- or 4-quart slow cooker with cooking spray. In the prepared cooker combine the rice and seasoning packets from rice mixes, milk, and apricots. Stir in butter until combined.

2 Cover and cook on low-heat setting for 2 hours or until rice is tender. Remove liner from cooker, if possible, or turn off cooker. Stir. Let stand, uncovered, about 30 minutes to cool slightly before serving.

3 To serve, stir well and spoon into dessert dishes. Top with toasted nuts.

***Note:** *To toast nuts, spread nuts in a single layer in a shallow baking pan. Bake in a 350°F oven for 5 to 10 minutes or until light golden brown, watching carefully and stirring once or twice so the nuts don't burn.*

Nutrition Facts per serving: 280 cal., 10 g total fat (4 g sat. fat), 21 mg chol., 214 mg sodium, 44 g carbo., 2 g fiber, 6 g pro.
Daily Values: 11% vit. A, 2% vit. C, 14% calcium, 6% iron

Gingerbread Pudding Cake

If you like warm and rich desserts, this pudding cake is sure to become one of your favorites. A scoop of vanilla ice cream melting on top adds more richness.

Prep: 15 minutes Cook: High 2 hours Stand: 45 minutes Makes: 8 servings

Nonstick cooking spray
1 14½-ounce package gingerbread mix
½ cup milk
½ cup raisins
2¼ cups water
¾ cup packed brown sugar
¾ cup butter or margarine
Vanilla ice cream (optional)

1 Lightly coat a 3½- or 4-quart slow cooker with cooking spray; set aside.

2 For batter, in a medium bowl stir gingerbread mix and milk together until moistened. Stir in raisins (batter will be thick). Spread gingerbread batter evenly in the bottom of the prepared cooker.

3 In a medium saucepan combine water, brown sugar, and butter; bring to boiling. Carefully pour mixture over batter in cooker.

4 Cover and cook on high-heat setting for 2 hours (center may appear moist but will set up upon standing). Remove liner from cooker, if possible, or turn off cooker. Let stand, uncovered, for 45 minutes to cool slightly before serving.

5 To serve, spoon warm cake into dessert dishes; spoon pudding that forms over cake. If desired, top with a scoop of vanilla ice cream.

Nutrition Facts per serving: 501 cal., 24 g total fat (13 g sat. fat), 50 mg chol., 548 mg sodium, 70 g carbo., 1 g fiber, 4 g pro.
Daily Values: 14% vit. A, 1% vit. C, 9% calcium, 19% iron

Brownie Pudding Cake

Thanks to pudding cake, you can have your cake and pudding too. Rich chocolate flavor runs through this soft cake-and-pudding blend. Serve it with ice cream or whipped cream.

Prep: 15 minutes Cook: High 2 hours Stand: 30 minutes Makes: 8 servings

Nonstick cooking spray
1 19.8-ounce package brownie mix
½ cup butter or margarine, melted
2 eggs
¼ cup water
¾ cup sugar
¾ cup unsweetened cocoa powder
3 cups boiling water
Vanilla ice cream (optional)

1 Lightly coat a 3½- or 4-quart slow cooker with cooking spray; set aside.

2 In a medium bowl stir together the brownie mix, melted butter, eggs, and the ¼ cup water until batter is nearly smooth. Spread brownie batter evenly in the bottom of the prepared cooker.

3 In another bowl combine the sugar and cocoa powder. Gradually stir the boiling water into the sugar-cocoa mixture. Pour evenly over batter in cooker.

4 Cover and cook on high-heat setting for 2 hours (center may appear moist but will set up upon standing). Remove liner from cooker, if possible, or turn off cooker. Let stand, uncovered, for 30 to 45 minutes to cool slightly before serving.

5 To serve, spoon warm cake into dessert dishes; spoon pudding over cake. If desired, top with a scoop of vanilla ice cream.

Nutrition Facts per serving: 534 cal., 25 g total fat (10 g sat. fat), 86 mg chol., 355 mg sodium, 76 g carbo., 0 g fiber, 6 g pro.
Daily Values: 11% vit. A, 11% calcium, 15% iron

Semisweet-Chocolate Bread Pudding

Have mugs of coffee and glasses of milk ready to accompany this one. Creamy bread pudding boasts rich semisweet chocolate flavor.

Prep: 20 minutes Cook: Low 2½ hours Stand: 30 minutes Makes: 8 servings

Nonstick cooking spray
3 cups milk
¾ cup semisweet chocolate pieces
¾ cup presweetened cocoa powder
3 eggs, slightly beaten
5 cups Hawaiian sweet bread or cinnamon swirl bread (no raisins) cut into ½-inch cubes, dried* (about 6½ ounces bread)
Whipped cream (optional)

1 Lightly coat a 3½- or 4-quart slow cooker with cooking spray; set aside.

2 In a medium saucepan bring milk to a simmer; remove saucepan from heat. Add chocolate pieces and presweetened cocoa powder (do not stir); let stand 5 minutes. Whisk until the chocolate is melted and smooth. Cool slightly (about 10 minutes). In a large mixing bowl whisk together the eggs and chocolate mixture. Gently stir in bread cubes. Pour mixture into the prepared cooker.

3 Cover and cook on low-heat setting about 2½ hours or until puffed and a knife inserted near center comes out clean. Remove liner from cooker, if possible, or turn off cooker. Let stand, uncovered, for 30 to 45 minutes to cool slightly before serving (pudding will fall as it cools).

4 To serve, spoon warm pudding into dessert dishes. If desired, top each serving with a dollop of whipped cream.

***Note:** *To make dry bread cubes, spread fresh bread cubes in a single layer in a 15×10×1-inch baking pan. Bake, uncovered, in a 300°F oven for 10 to 15 minutes or until dry, stirring twice; cool.*

Nutrition Facts per serving: 360 cal., 12 g total fat (6 g sat. fat), 95 mg chol., 214 mg sodium, 62 g carbo., 4 g fiber, 9 g pro.
Daily Values: 8% vit. A, 2% vit. C, 15% calcium, 15% iron

Pumpkin Custard Bread Pudding

Serve bread pudding instead of pie for a change this Thanksgiving. Chopped pecans complement the custardlike texture.

Prep: 15 minutes Cook: 3½ hours Stand: 30 minutes Makes: 8 servings

Nonstick cooking spray
2 eggs, beaten
⅔ cup half-and-half or light cream
1 30-ounce can pumpkin pie filling mix (with sugar and spices)
7 cups bread cut into ½-inch cubes, dried* (5 cups dry)
½ cup chopped pecans
Caramel ice cream topping (optional)

1 Lightly coat a 3½- or 4-quart slow cooker with cooking spray; set aside.

2 In a large mixing bowl whisk together the eggs and half-and-half. Stir in the pumpkin pie mix until combined. Stir in bread cubes. Pour mixture into prepared cooker.

3 Cover and cook on low-heat setting for 3½ to 4 hours or until a knife inserted near center comes out clean (160°F). Remove liner from cooker, if possible, or turn off cooker. Let stand, uncovered, for 30 to 45 minutes to cool slightly before serving.

4 To serve, spoon bread pudding into dessert dishes; sprinkle each serving with some nuts. If desired, drizzle with caramel ice cream topping.

***Note:** *To make 5 cups dry bread cubes, you'll need about 8 or 9 slices fresh bread. Spread bread cubes in a single layer in a 15×10×1-inch baking pan. Bake, uncovered, in a 300°F oven for 10 to 15 minutes or until dry, stirring twice; cool.*

Nutrition Facts per serving: 268 cal., 9 g total fat (2 g sat. fat), 61 mg chol., 379 mg sodium, 42 g carbo., 10 g fiber, 6 g pro.
Daily Values: 180% vit. A, 7% vit. C, 10% calcium, 12% iron

Apple Pie Bread Pudding

Apple pie filling and cinnamon-raisin bread star in this luscious dessert. If you don't have cinnamon-raisin bread, use white bread, 1/3 cup raisins, and 1/8 teaspoon cinnamon.

Prep: 10 minutes Cook: Low 3 hours Stand: 30 minutes Makes: 6 servings

- Nonstick cooking spray
- 3 eggs, beaten
- 2 cups milk, half-and-half, or light cream
- ½ cup sugar
- 1 21-ounce can chunky apple pie filling (more fruit)
- 6½ cups cinnamon-raisin bread cut into ½-inch cubes, dried* (4½ cups dry)
- Whipped cream or vanilla ice cream (optional)

1 Lightly coat a 3½- or 4-quart slow cooker with cooking spray; set aside.

2 In a large mixing bowl whisk together the eggs, milk, and sugar. Gently stir in pie filling and bread cubes. Pour mixture into prepared cooker.

3 Cover and cook on low-heat setting for 3 hours until a knife inserted near center comes out clean (mixture will be puffed). Remove liner from cooker, if possible, or turn off cooker. Let stand, uncovered, for 30 to 45 minutes to cool slightly before serving (pudding will fall as it cools).

4 To serve, spoon bread pudding into dessert dishes. If desired, top each serving with a dollop of whipped cream or a scoop of vanilla ice cream.

***Note:** *To make 4½ cups dry bread cubes, you'll need 8 or 9 slices fresh bread. Spread bread cubes in a single layer in a 15×10×1-inch baking pan. Bake, uncovered, in a 300°F oven for 10 to 15 minutes or until dry, stirring twice; cool.*

Nutrition Facts per serving: 548 cal., 6 g total fat (2 g sat. fat), 113 mg chol., 133 mg sodium, 114 g carbo., 8 g fiber, 16 g pro.
Daily Values: 7% vit. A, 5% vit. C, 15% calcium, 24% iron

Poached Pears in Cran-Amaretto Sauce

When dessert has to be special, this cranberry-pear combination fits the bill.

Prep: 25 minutes Cook: Low 4 hours, High 2 hours Stand: 30 minutes Makes: 6 servings

1½ cups cranberries
⅔ cup water
½ cup sugar
⅓ cup amaretto or hazelnut liqueur
6 ripe medium pears, peeled, cored, and halved
Vanilla ice cream (optional)
Sliced almonds, toasted* (optional)

1 In a 3½- or 4-quart slow cooker combine cranberries, water, sugar, and amaretto. Add pears, stirring to coat.

2 Cover and cook on low-heat setting for 4 to 5 hours or on high-heat setting for 2 to 2½ hours. Remove liner from cooker, if possible, or turn off cooker. Let stand, uncovered, for 30 minutes to cool slightly before serving.

3 To serve, divide cranberry sauce among 6 dessert plates; place 2 pear halves on each plate. If desired, serve with ice cream and garnish with toasted almonds.

***Note:** *To toast nuts, spread nuts in a single layer in a shallow baking pan. Bake in a 350°F oven for 5 to 10 minutes or until light golden brown, watching carefully and stirring once or twice so the nuts don't burn.*

Nutrition Facts per serving: 241 cal., 4 g total fat (0 g sat. fat), 0 mg chol., 1 mg sodium, 49 g carbo., 6 g fiber, 2 g pro.
Daily Values: 1% vit. A, 14% vit. C, 3% calcium, 4% iron

Apricot-Peach Dessert Soup

A light, fresh finish to a heavy meal, this cinnamon-scented soup shows off its pretty color when served in glass dessert bowls.

Prep: 15 minutes Cook: Low 5 hours, High 2½ hours Stand: 30 minutes Makes: 10 servings

- 4 cups orange-peach-mango juice or orange-tangerine juice
- 1 16-ounce package frozen unsweetened peach slices
- 1 7-ounce package dried apricots, cut into 1-inch pieces
- 1 6-ounce package dried cherries and golden raisins
- 6 inches stick cinnamon

1 In a 3½- or 4-quart slow cooker combine the orange-peach-mango juice, frozen peaches, dried apricots, dried cherries and raisins, and cinnamon.

2 Cover and cook on low-heat setting for 5 to 6 hours or on high-heat setting for 2½ to 3 hours. Remove liner from cooker, if possible, or turn off cooker. Let stand, uncovered, for 30 to 45 minutes to cool slightly before serving. Remove stick cinnamon with a slotted spoon and discard.

Nutrition Facts per serving: 167 cal., 0 g total fat (0 g sat. fat), 0 mg chol., 11 mg sodium, 42 g carbo., 3 g fiber, 2 g pro.
Daily Values: 19% vit. A, 46% vit. C, 3% calcium, 4% iron

Cream-Topped Pears in Orange Sauce

Orange juice and marmalade render a pretty syrup in which the pear halves cook. Whipped cream adds a rich note and a pretty garnish.

Prep: 15 minutes Cook: Low 4 hours, High 2 hours Stand: 30 minutes Makes: 8 servings

- ¾ cup orange juice
- 6 tablespoons orange marmalade
- 2 teaspoons quick-cooking tapioca
- 8 small to medium firm ripe pears, peeled, cored, and quartered
- 1 cup whipping cream

1 In a 3½- or 4-quart slow cooker combine orange juice, 4 tablespoons of the marmalade, and the tapioca. Add pears. Toss gently to coat.

2 Cover and cook on low-heat setting for 4 to 5 hours or on high-heat setting for 2 to 2½ hours. Remove liner from cooker, if possible, or turn off cooker. Let stand, uncovered, for 30 minutes to cool slightly before serving.

3 In a chilled medium bowl combine whipping cream and remaining 2 tablespoons marmalade; beat until soft peaks form.

4 To serve, spoon pears and orange sauce into dessert dishes. Top with whipped cream mixture.

Nutrition Facts per serving: 221 cal., 12 g total fat (7 g sat. fat), 41 mg chol., 20 mg sodium, 31 g carbo., 3 g fiber, 1 g pro. Daily Values: 10% vit. A, 28% vit. C, 4% calcium, 2% iron

8

Bonus: 5-Ingredient Side Dish Go-Alongs

Flaky Biscuits

Self-rising flour is the key to these Sunday-best biscuits. The flour has salt and some leavening already added.

Prep: 15 minutes Bake: 10 minutes Oven: 425°F Makes: 10 to 12 biscuits

- 2 cups self-rising flour*
- 1/4 teaspoon baking soda
- 1/4 cup butter or margarine
- 3/4 cup buttermilk

1 In a medium bowl stir together flour and baking soda. With a pastry blender or 2 knives cut in butter until mixture resembles coarse crumbs. Make a well in center. Add the buttermilk all at once; stir until moistened.

2 Turn dough out onto a lightly floured surface. Quickly knead dough by gently folding and pressing the dough for 10 to 12 strokes or until nearly smooth. Pat or lightly roll dough to 1/2-inch thickness. Cut dough into circles with a floured 2 1/2-inch biscuit cutter.

3 Place biscuits 1 inch apart on a lightly greased baking sheet. Bake in a 425° oven for 10 to 15 minutes or until golden. Remove biscuits from baking sheet and serve hot.

***Note:** *If you can't find self-rising flour at your supermarket, substitute 2 cups all-purpose flour plus 2 teaspoons baking powder, 1 teaspoon salt, and 1/2 teaspoon baking soda.*

Nutrition Facts per biscuit: 139 cal., 5 g total fat (3 g sat. fat), 14 mg chol., 418 mg sodium, 19 g carbo., 1 g fiber, 3 g pro.
Daily Values: 4% vit. A, 11% calcium, 7% iron

Pepper-Cheese Biscuits: *Prepare biscuits as above, except stir 3/4 cup shredded Monterey Jack cheese with jalapeño peppers (3 ounces), 2 tablespoons snipped fresh chives, and 1/8 teaspoon cayenne pepper into flour and butter mixture.*

Rosemary and Swiss Buns

No one will ever guess that these delicious buns start with a hot roll mix. You can vary the herb and the cheese; next time try oregano and shredded cheddar.

Prep: 25 minutes Rise: 30 minutes Bake: 12 minutes Oven: 375°F Makes: 12 buns

- 1 16-ounce package hot roll mix
- ¾ cup shredded Swiss cheese (3 ounces)
- 2 small onions, thinly sliced and separated into rings (⅔ cup)
- 1 tablespoon snipped fresh rosemary or 1 teaspoon dried rosemary, crushed
- 1 tablespoon cooking oil

1 Grease 2 large baking sheets; set aside. Prepare hot roll mix according to package directions, except stir in Swiss cheese with the liquid called for in package directions. Continue with package directions through the kneading and resting steps. After dough rests, divide into 12 equal portions and shape into balls. On a lightly floured surface roll each ball into a 4-inch round. Place on prepared baking sheets. Cover and set aside.

2 In a medium skillet cook and stir onions and rosemary in hot oil until onion is tender. Using your fingertips, make ½-inch-deep indentations on the surface of the dough rounds. Spoon the onion mixture into the indentations. Cover and let rise in a warm place until nearly double (30 to 40 minutes).

3 Bake in a 375° oven for 12 to 15 minutes or until golden. Transfer buns to a wire rack and cool completely. To store, place buns in an airtight container or bag, or wrap in foil, and store in refrigerator for up to 3 days or freeze for up to 1 month.

Nutrition Facts per bun: 200 cal., 6 g total fat (1 g sat. fat), 23 mg chol., 265 mg sodium, 30 g carbo., 0 g fiber, 7 g pro.
Daily Values: 1% vit. A, 1% vit. C, 7% calcium, 6% iron

Have-a-Ball Rolls

Ordinary frozen bread dough becomes something special when you shape it into tiny balls and top them with crunchy seeds.

Prep: 20 minutes Rise: 30 minutes Bake: 13 minutes Oven: 350°F Makes: 30 to 36 mini rolls

- 1 16-ounce loaf frozen white or whole wheat bread dough, thawed
- 1 egg white
- 1 tablespoon water
- Fennel seeds, mustard seeds, and/or dill seeds

1 Lightly grease a baking sheet or 30 to 36 1¾-inch muffin cups; set aside.

2 Divide dough into 30 to 36 pieces. Shape into small balls. Place rolls on prepared baking sheet or in prepared cups. Cover and let rise until nearly double in size (about 30 minutes).

3 Beat together the egg white and water. Brush mixture over the rolls. Sprinkle generously with desired seeds. Bake in a 350° oven for 13 to 15 minutes or until golden brown. Transfer rolls to wire racks. Serve warm.

Nutrition Facts per mini roll: 37 cal., 0 g total fat (0 g sat. fat), 0 mg chol., 2 mg sodium, 7 g carbo., 0 g fiber, 1 g pro.
Daily Values: 2% calcium, 1% iron

Green Onion Parker House Biscuits

Refrigerated biscuit dough and softened herb-blend cheese make these biscuits as quick to prepare as they are tasty.

Prep: 10 minutes Bake: 8 minutes Oven: 400°F Makes: 10 biscuits

- 1 5.2-ounce container semisoft cheese with garlic and herb, such as Boursin
- ¼ cup sliced green onions (2)
- 1 12-ounce package (10) refrigerated biscuits
- 1 egg yolk
- 1 tablespoon water
- 2 tablespoons grated Parmesan cheese
- Sliced green onions (optional)

1 In a small bowl stir together the cheese and the ¼ cup green onions; set aside.

2 Unwrap biscuits. Using your fingers, gently split the biscuits horizontally. (Some refrigerated doughs will need to be sliced.) Place the biscuit bottoms on a greased baking sheet. Spread about 1 tablespoon of the cheese mixture over each biscuit bottom. Replace biscuit tops.

3 In a small bowl use a fork to beat together egg yolk and water. Brush biscuit tops with yolk mixture. Sprinkle with Parmesan cheese and, if desired, additional sliced green onions. Bake in a 400° oven for 8 to 10 minutes or until golden brown. Serve warm.

Nutrition Facts per biscuit: 149 cal., 8 g total fat (5 g sat. fat), 23 mg chol., 394 mg sodium, 16 g carbo., 0 g fiber, 4 g pro.
Daily Values: 1% vit. A, 1% vit. C, 2% calcium, 6% iron

Really Red Coleslaw

Red ingredients make this a memorable coleslaw combination. Use only a vinegar-and-oil-based dressing.

Prep: 15 minutes Chill: up to 6 hours Makes: 8 servings

- 1 10-ounce package shredded red cabbage (about 6 cups)
- 1 medium red onion, slivered (1 cup)
- ½ cup dried tart red cherries
- ½ cup bottled raspberry vinaigrette salad dressing
- 1 tablespoon seedless red raspberry preserves

1 In a large bowl combine cabbage, red onion, and dried cherries; set aside.

2 In a small bowl combine salad dressing and preserves; pour over cabbage mixture and toss to coat. Serve at room temperature or chill up to 6 hours.

Nutrition Facts per serving: 108 cal., 6 g total fat (1 g sat. fat), 0 mg chol., 5 mg sodium, 12 g carbo., 1 g fiber, 1 g pro.
Daily Values: 1% vit. A, 36% vit. C, 2% calcium, 1% iron

Fresh Corn-Rice Salad

For an even simpler recipe, substitute 2 cups frozen whole kernel corn and cook according to package directions.

Prep: 20 minutes Cook: 4 minutes Makes: 6 servings

- 4 fresh ears of corn
- 1½ cups cooked rice, cooled
- 1 10- to 14½-ounce can diced tomatoes and green chile peppers, undrained
- 2 tablespoons shredded radish

1 Husk ears of corn and remove silks with a stiff brush; rinse. Cut kernels from cob* (you should have about 2 cups of kernels).

2 In a medium saucepan cook corn, covered, in a small amount of boiling salted water for 4 minutes. Drain. Mix with rice. Stir in undrained tomatoes. Sprinkle with radish. Serve at room temperature.

*Note: *To remove the corn kernels, hold the cob at the top and slice downward with a sharp knife onto a cutting board. Repeat, turning cob until you've captured every kernel.*

Nutrition Facts per serving: 123 cal., 1 g total fat (0 g sat. fat), 0 mg chol., 332 mg sodium, 28 g carbo., 2 g fiber, 3 g pro.
Daily Values: 12% vit. A, 16% vit. C, 2% calcium, 6% iron

Mediterranean-Style Pasta Salad

The kalamata olives in this salad have a pungent but pleasant flavor. If you can't find them in the supermarket, use another type of ripe olive.

Prep: 25 minutes Chill: 4 hours Makes: 4 or 5 servings

1½ cups dried mostaccioli pasta
1 cup halved cherry tomatoes or grape tomatoes
⅓ cup sliced pitted kalamata or other ripe olives
1 4-ounce package crumbled feta cheese
½ cup bottled balsamic vinaigrette salad dressing

1 Cook the pasta according to package directions; drain. Rinse with cold water; drain well.

2 In a large bowl combine the cooked pasta, tomatoes, olives, cheese, and salad dressing. Toss to coat. Cover and chill for 4 to 8 hours. Stir gently before serving.

Nutrition Facts per serving: 335 cal., 17 g total fat (5 g sat. fat), 25 mg chol., 792 mg sodium, 36 g carbo., 2 g fiber, 9 g pro.
Daily Values: 8% vit. A, 14% vit. C, 15% calcium, 8% iron

Marinated Bean Salad

The flavors of molasses and balsamic vinegar mingle beautifully in this side-dish salad.

Prep: 20 minutes Chill: 4 hours Makes: 8 servings

- 8 ounces fresh green beans, trimmed and cut into bite-size pieces, or one 9-ounce package frozen cut green beans
- 2 15- to 19-ounce cans navy, red kidney, and/or cannellini beans (white kidney beans), rinsed and drained
- ½ cup thinly sliced red onion
- ½ cup bottled balsamic vinaigrette salad dressing
- 3 tablespoons molasses

1 In a medium saucepan cook the fresh green beans in lightly salted boiling water for 7 to 10 minutes or until just tender; drain. (If using frozen green beans, cook according to package directions; drain.) Rinse beans with cold water; drain again.

2 In a large bowl stir together the green beans, canned beans, and onion. In a small bowl stir together the dressing and molasses. Pour over bean mixture and toss to coat. Cover; chill in refrigerator for 4 to 24 hours. Serve with a slotted spoon.

Nutrition Facts per serving: 196 cal., 5 g total fat (1 g sat. fat), 0 mg chol., 656 mg sodium, 31 g carbo., 6 g fiber, 9 g pro.
Daily Values: 3% vit. A, 7% vit. C, 8% calcium, 14% iron

Fruity Wild Rice Salad

Regardless of its name, wild rice is not rice at all. It's a marsh grass, which is why it takes almost three times as long to cook as white rice does.

Prep: 50 minutes Chill: 4 hours Makes: 6 servings

- ⅔ cup uncooked wild rice
- ½ cup dried cranberries
- ⅓ cup sliced green onions (3)
- ½ cup bottled raspberry vinaigrette salad dressing or other vinaigrette salad dressing
- ½ cup coarsely chopped pecans, toasted*

1 Rinse wild rice in a strainer under cold running water. Cook according to package directions until tender; drain if necessary.

2 In a medium bowl stir together the rice, cranberries, green onions, and salad dressing. Cover and chill for 4 to 24 hours. Stir in pecans before serving.

***Note:** *To toast nuts, spread nuts in a single layer in a shallow baking pan. Bake in a 350°F oven for 5 to 10 minutes or until light golden brown, watching carefully and stirring once or twice so the nuts don't burn.*

Nutrition Facts per serving: 186 cal., 7 g total fat (1 g sat. fat), 0 mg chol., 275 mg sodium, 30 g carbo., 3 g fiber, 4 g pro.
Daily Values: 1% vit. A, 2% vit. C, 1% calcium, 4% iron

Fruit and Broccoli Salad

Shredded broccoli slaw mix, one of many convenience foods found in modern supermarkets, helps you put this zippy salad together in a flash.

Prep: 15 minutes Chill: 1 hour Makes: 12 to 16 servings

- 1 16-ounce package shredded broccoli (broccoli slaw mix)
- 2 cups seedless red and/or green grapes, halved
- 2 medium apples, cored and chopped
- ⅔ cup bottled citrus salad dressing, such as tangerine vinaigrette
- 1 cup coarsely chopped pecans or walnuts, toasted if desired*

1 In a very large bowl combine shredded broccoli, grapes, and apples.

2 Up to 1 hour before serving, pour salad dressing over broccoli mixture; toss to coat. Cover and chill. Transfer to a serving bowl. Toss in nuts before serving.

***Note:** *To toast nuts, spread nuts in a single layer in a shallow baking pan. Bake in a 350°F oven for 5 to 10 minutes or until light golden brown, watching carefully and stirring once or twice so the nuts don't burn.*

Nutrition Facts per serving: 219 cal., 15 g total fat (2 g sat. fat), 6 mg chol., 131 mg sodium, 21 g carbo., 2 g fiber, 3 g pro.
Daily Values: 8% vit. A, 32% vit. C, 3% calcium, 5% iron

Shredded Hash Browns

Sleepy hash browns with onions receive a wake-up call with the addition of zippy jalapeños.

Prep: 10 minutes Cook: 13 minutes Makes: 2 or 3 servings

- 3 to 4 small russet or white potatoes (about 12 ounces)
- ¼ cup finely chopped onion
- 1 small fresh jalapeño pepper, banana pepper, or Anaheim chile pepper, seeded and chopped (optional)*
- ¼ teaspoon salt
- ⅛ teaspoon coarsely ground black pepper
- 2 tablespoons butter, cooking oil, or margarine

1 Peel potatoes and coarsely shred using the coarsest side of the grater (you should have about 2 cups). Rinse shredded potatoes in a colander; drain well and pat dry. In a medium bowl combine shredded potatoes, onion, jalapeño pepper (if using), salt, and black pepper.

2 In a large nonstick skillet heat butter over medium heat for 1 to 2 minutes or until hot. Carefully add potatoes, pressing into an even pancakelike round (about 7 to 8 inches in diameter). Using a spatula, press mixture firmly. Cook, covered, over medium heat for 8 minutes or until golden brown. Check occasionally and reduce heat, if necessary, to prevent overbrowning. Turn using two spatulas or a spatula and fork. (If you're not sure you can turn it in a single flip, cut into quarters and turn by sections.) Cook, uncovered, 5 to 7 minutes more or until golden brown and crisp. Remove from skillet; cut into wedges.

***Note:** *Because hot chile peppers, such as jalapeños, contain volatile oils that can burn your skin and eyes, avoid direct contact with chiles as much as possible. When working with chile peppers, wear plastic or rubber gloves. If your bare hands do touch the chile peppers, wash your hands well with soap and water.*

Nutrition Facts per serving: 168 cal., 9 g total fat (1 g sat. fat), 0 mg chol., 197 mg sodium, 19 g carbo., 2 g fiber, 3 g pro.
Daily Values: 27% vit. C, 1% calcium, 5% iron

Sour Cream Smashed Potatoes

These creamy, flavorful potatoes are a great accompaniment for a slow-cooked beef or pork roast. Check out the make-ahead directions for extra convenience.

Prep: 20 minutes Cook: 20 minutes Makes: 6 servings

4 medium baking potatoes (about 1⅓ pounds)
4 cloves garlic, peeled
½ cup dairy sour cream
2 to 3 tablespoons milk (optional)
Salt and black pepper
1 tablespoon finely shredded Parmesan cheese (optional)

1 Peel potatoes, if desired. Cook potatoes and garlic cloves, covered, in boiling water for 20 to 25 minutes or until potatoes are tender; drain.

2 In a large bowl mash potatoes and garlic with a potato masher; add sour cream. If necessary, beat in enough milk to make fluffy. Season to taste with salt and pepper.* Return potatoes to pan and heat through. Transfer potatoes to a serving bowl. If desired, sprinkle with Parmesan cheese.

Nutrition Facts per serving: 110 cal., 4 g total fat (2 g sat. fat), 7 mg chol., 109 mg sodium, 17 g carbo., 2 g fiber, 3 g pro.
Daily Values: 3% vit. A, 24% vit. C, 3% calcium, 5% iron

***To make ahead:** *Prepare potatoes as directed, except place in a greased 1½-quart casserole before heating through. Cover and chill up to 24 hours. Bake, covered, in a 350°F oven for 55 minutes or until heated through. If desired, sprinkle with Parmesan cheese just before serving.*

Veggie Mash

This is mashed potatoes with a few friends thrown in. It's wonderful partnered with slow-cooked beef or pork roast.

Prep: 15 minutes Cook: 15 minutes Makes: 6 servings

- 6 medium carrots, sliced (3 cups)
- 4 medium red potatoes (1¼ pounds), scrubbed and cubed
- 1 cup coarsely chopped broccoli
- ½ of an 8-ounce container dairy sour cream French onion dip
- ½ teaspoon seasoned pepper

1 In a Dutch oven or large saucepan cook the carrots and potatoes, covered, in boiling water for 15 minutes or until tender, adding broccoli the last 3 minutes of cooking time. Drain vegetables; return to pan.

2 Mash with a potato masher or beat with an electric mixer on low speed. Add dip and seasoned pepper. Beat until fluffy. Spoon into a serving bowl.

Nutrition Facts per serving: 146 cal., 3 g total fat (2 g sat. fat), 0 mg chol., 173 mg sodium, 27 g carbo., 5 g fiber, 4 g pro.
Daily Values: 387% vit. A, 51% vit. C, 4% calcium, 7% iron

Sweet Saucy Carrots and Pecans

No peeling required! This versatile side dish starts with a package of peeled baby carrots, leaving the cook more time to focus on the main meal.

Start to Finish: 20 minutes Makes: 4 servings

- 1 pound peeled baby carrots
- 2 tablespoons orange marmalade
- 1 tablespoon butter or margarine
- ½ teaspoon salt
- 2 tablespoons pecan pieces, toasted*

1 In a large saucepan cook the carrots, covered, in a small amount of boiling water for 8 to 10 minutes or until crisp-tender. Drain. Return carrots to pan.

2 Add the orange marmalade, butter, and salt. Stir until carrots are coated. Top with the pecans.

***Note:** *To toast nuts, spread nuts in a single layer in a shallow baking pan. Bake in a 350°F oven for 5 to 10 minutes or until light golden brown, watching carefully and stirring once or twice so the nuts don't burn.*

Nutrition Facts per serving: 124 cal., 6 g total fat (2 g sat. fat), 8 mg chol., 365 mg sodium, 19 g carbo., 4 g fiber, 2 g pro.
Daily Values: 577% vit. A, 13% vit. C, 4% calcium, 4% iron

Summer Squash with Peppers

Brighten your table by taking advantage of the range of colors of sweet peppers. Choose from green, red, yellow, or orange.

Prep: 15 minutes Roast: 15 minutes Oven: 425°F Makes: 6 servings

- 2 pounds zucchini and/or yellow summer squash, cut into bite-size chunks
- 1 green or red sweet pepper, cut into strips
- 2 tablespoons olive oil
- 1½ teaspoons Greek-style or Mediterranean-style seasoning blend
- ¼ teaspoon black pepper

1 Place the squash pieces and sweet pepper strips in a large shallow roasting pan. Drizzle with oil. Sprinkle with seasoning and black pepper; toss to coat.

2 Roast, uncovered, in a 425° oven for 15 minutes or until just tender; stir once.

Nutrition Facts per serving: 66 cal., 5 g total fat (1 g sat. fat), 0 mg chol., 25 mg sodium, 6 g carbo., 2 g fiber, 2 g pro.
Daily Values: 30% vit. A, 69% vit. C, 2% calcium, 4% iron

Mediterranean Parsnips

Another time, try cooked baby carrots or quartered baby red potatoes in place of the parsnips.

Prep: 25 minutes Cook: 7 minutes Makes: 8 servings

- 3½ pounds small parsnips
- 3 tablespoons olive oil
- ¼ teaspoon each salt and black pepper
- 1 cup pitted kalamata olives, coarsely chopped
- ½ cup capers, drained (3½-ounce jar)

1 Peel and slice the parsnips lengthwise into ¼-inch slices. In a large saucepan cook parsnips, covered, in a small amount of boiling lightly salted water for 7 to 9 minutes or until tender; drain.

2 Gently toss parsnips with olive oil, salt, and pepper. Transfer to a serving dish. Top with olives and capers. Serve immediately.

Nutrition Facts per serving: 234 cal., 8 g total fat (1 g sat. fat), 0 mg chol., 535 mg sodium, 41 g carbo., 9 g fiber, 3 g pro.
Daily Values: 44% vit. C, 8% calcium, 7% iron

Caramel Clementines

Clementines, tangerines, satsuma oranges, and dancy tangerines are different types of mandarin oranges, and you can use them interchangeably in this recipe.

Prep: 10 minutes Cook: 20 minutes Makes: 6 servings

- 6 clementines or other mandarin orange variety
- 1 14½-ounce can apricot nectar (1¾ cups)
- ½ cup sugar
- Dash cayenne pepper (optional)
- 2 tablespoons Southern Comfort, orange liqueur, or orange juice

1 Peel clementines and remove the fibrous strands of pith from the fruit. In a medium saucepan place clementines, apricot nectar, sugar, and, if desired, cayenne pepper. Bring to boiling; reduce heat. Cover and simmer for 5 minutes. Using a slotted spoon, transfer fruit to six individual dessert dishes.

2 Continue to gently boil apricot nectar mixture about 15 minutes or until thick and syrupy. Remove from heat. Stir Southern Comfort into syrupy mixture. Spoon over fruit. Serve warm.

Nutrition Facts per serving: 151 cal., 0 g total fat (0 g sat. fat), 0 mg chol., 3 mg sodium, 36 g carbo., 2 g fiber, 1 g pro.
Daily Values: 35% vit. A, 44% vit. C, 2% calcium, 2% iron

Mocha Pears

Prepare the pears and syrup for this dessert early in the day and chill. To serve, dollop with yogurt and sprinkle with mini chocolate pieces.

Prep: 10 minutes Cook: 15 minutes Chill: 4 hours Makes: 6 servings

2 16-ounce cans or one 29-ounce can pear halves in heavy syrup (12 pear halves)
2 teaspoons instant coffee crystals
1 teaspoon vanilla
¾ cup vanilla low-fat yogurt
Miniature semisweet chocolate pieces

1 Drain pears, reserving syrup. Place pears in a bowl; set aside. In a saucepan combine reserved syrup and coffee crystals. Bring to boiling; reduce heat. Simmer, uncovered, about 15 minutes or until mixture is slightly thickened and reduced to ½ cup. Stir in vanilla. Pour coffee mixture over pears. Cover and chill in the refrigerator at least 4 hours, turning pears once.

2 To serve, use a slotted spoon to place 2 pear halves into each of 6 individual dessert dishes. Drizzle with the reserved coffee mixture. Top with yogurt and chocolate pieces.

Nutrition Facts per serving: 168 cal., 2 g total fat (1 g sat. fat), 2 mg chol., 30 mg sodium, 37 g carbo., 3 g fiber, 2 g pro.
Daily Values: 1% vit. A, 3% vit. C, 6% calcium, 3% iron

Trio of Fast Fruit Desserts

If you're looking for single-serving dessert ideas, check out one of these three desserts. Double or triple the ingredients for more servings.

Start to Finish: 10 minutes per dessert

- ¼ cup prepared vanilla custard, vanilla pudding, or tapioca pudding
- ½ cup pitted dark sweet cherries, halved
- Cherry liqueur, such as kirsch

Mound custard in a chilled dessert bowl. Spoon cherries over custard. Drizzle with a cherry liqueur. Makes 1 serving.

Nutrition Facts per serving: 150 cal., 2 g total fat (1 g sat. fat), 5 mg chol., 111 mg sodium, 28 g carbo., 2 g fiber, 3 g pro.
Daily Values: 5% vit. A, 9% vit. C, 9% calcium, 2% iron

- ⅓ cup vanilla or peach-flavored frozen yogurt or ice cream
- ½ ripe nectarine or peach, pitted and sliced
- Crumbled amaretti cookies or gingersnaps

Scoop frozen yogurt into a chilled dessert bowl. Add nectarine slices and sprinkle with cookies. Makes 1 serving.

Nutrition Facts per serving: 161 cal., 4 g total fat (2 g sat. fat), 10 mg chol., 33 mg sodium, 28 g carbo., 1 g fiber, 3 g pro.
Daily Values: 11% vit. A, 6% vit. C, 7% calcium, 1% iron

- 2 mangoes, peeled, seeded, and sliced
- ¼ cup light cream cheese, softened
- 2 tablespoons white grape juice or orange juice
- Chopped pistachios

Divide mango slices between 2 chilled dessert bowls. In mixing bowl beat cheese and juice together. Spoon over fruit. Top with pistachios. Makes 2 servings.

Nutrition Facts per serving: 305 cal., 13 g total fat (4 g sat. fat), 17 mg chol., 95 mg sodium, 44 g carbo., 5 g fiber, 8 g pro.
Daily Values: 167% vit. A, 104% vit. C, 7% calcium, 8% iron

Fast and Fruity Banana Split Tarts

After a hearty meal, serve a mini dessert. Let your family decide whether one or two of these mini tarts qualify as one portion.

Start to Finish: 10 minutes Makes: 15 tarts

- 1 8-ounce tub cream cheese with pineapple
- ¼ cup strawberry preserves
- 1 2.1-ounce package baked miniature phyllo dough shells (15)
- 1 small banana, thinly sliced
- 3 tablespoons chocolate ice cream topping

1 For filling, in a small mixing bowl beat the cream cheese and preserves with an electric mixer on medium speed until light and fluffy. Spoon filling into each phyllo shell. If desired, cover and chill in the refrigerator for up to 4 hours.

2 To serve, divide banana slices among shells. Drizzle with ice cream topping. Serve immediately.

Nutrition Facts per tart: 105 cal., 5 g total fat (3 g sat. fat), 12 mg chol., 65 mg sodium, 13 g carbo., 0 g fiber, 1 g pro.
Daily Values: 3% vit. A, 2% vit. C, 2% calcium, 1% iron

Dessert Waffles with Raspberry Coulis

Think outside the box. A breakfast favorite becomes dessert when paired with a mouthwatering raspberry sauce (called coulis) and ice cream.

Start to Finish: 10 minutes Makes: 6 servings

- 1 10-ounce package frozen raspberries in syrup, thawed
- ¼ cup sifted powdered sugar
- 2 tablespoons crème de cassis (optional)
- 6 frozen waffles, toasted
- 3 cups vanilla ice cream

1 For coulis, press raspberries and syrup through a fine-mesh sieve; discard seeds. In small bowl combine sieved berries, the sugar, and, if desired, crème de cassis.

2 To serve, cut each toasted waffle diagonally in half. Place 2 waffle halves on each of 6 dessert plates; top with vanilla ice cream. Drizzle with coulis.

Nutrition Facts per serving: 361 cal., 15 g total fat (8 g sat. fat), 79 mg chol., 381 mg sodium, 54 g carbo., 2 g fiber, 5 g pro.
Daily Values: 18% vit. A, 7% vit. C, 16% calcium, 12% iron

Mango Cream

Whip this creamy dessert together just before serving, or for convenience, chill it up to 4 hours.

Prep: 20 minutes Chill: up to 4 hours Makes: 6 servings

- 1 26-ounce jar refrigerated mango slices, drained
- 3 tablespoons sugar
- 1 tablespoon lemon juice
- 1 cup whipping cream
- 2 oranges, peeled and sectioned

1 Place mango in a blender or food processor. Cover and blend or process until smooth. Add 2 tablespoons of sugar and the lemon juice; cover and blend or process until combined. Transfer mixture to a medium bowl; set aside.

2 In a mixing bowl combine whipping cream and the remaining 1 tablespoon sugar. Beat with an electric mixer on low speed until soft peaks form. Fold cream into mango mixture. Spoon into 6 glasses or dessert dishes; top with orange sections. Cover and chill in the refrigerator for up to 4 hours.

Nutrition Facts per serving: 281 cal., 15 g total fat (9 g sat. fat), 55 mg chol., 20 mg sodium, 37 g carbo., 1 g fiber, 1 g pro.
Daily Values: 28% vit. A, 110% vit. C, 4% calcium, 4% iron

Icy Orange-Filled Cupcakes

With some minor surgery, purchased cupcakes go from bland to grand.

Prep: 20 minutes Freeze: 3 hours Makes: 6 cupcakes

1 pint frozen vanilla yogurt
¼ cup frozen orange juice concentrate
6 purchased frosted yellow cupcakes

1 Line a 9-inch pie plate with foil; set aside. Soften half the frozen yogurt in a chilled bowl by pressing it against the sides of the bowl with a wooden spoon. Spread the softened frozen yogurt in prepared pie plate. Cover with plastic wrap and freeze about 1 hour or until firm.

2 In a chilled bowl combine the remaining half of the frozen yogurt and the orange juice concentrate. Stir with a wooden spoon until frozen yogurt is softened and mixture is smooth. Remove plastic wrap from yogurt layer in pie plate. Spread orange mixture over plain vanilla yogurt layer. Cover with plastic wrap and freeze 2 hours or until yogurt layers are firm.

3 Remove paper liners from cupcakes, if present; set aside. Slice cupcakes in half horizontally. Remove plastic wrap from layered frozen yogurt. Lift the layered frozen yogurt from plate using the foil. With a 2- to 2½-inch round scalloped cutter (depending on size of cupcakes), cut out 6 rounds from layered frozen yogurt. (Return remaining frozen yogurt to freezer for another use.)

4 Place a round of frozen yogurt between cupcake halves. Return to reserved paper liners, if using.

Nutrition Facts per cupcake: 232 cal., 6 g total fat (2 g sat. fat), 6 mg chol., 138 mg sodium, 41 g carbo., 0 g fiber, 3 g pro.
Daily Values: 4% vit. A, 30% vit. C, 26% calcium, 2% iron

Frozen Chocolate-Peanut Dessert

If you want to mix it up, next time substitute your favorite ice cream flavors for the chocolate or vanilla ice cream.

Prep: 25 minutes Stand: 10 minutes Freeze: 15 minutes plus 4 hours Makes: 15 servings

30 chocolate with white filling sandwich cookies, coarsely crushed
¼ cup butter, melted
½ gallon vanilla or chocolate ice cream
1 cup peanuts
1 12-ounce jar chocolate fudge ice cream topping (about 1 cup)
1 banana, sliced (optional)
Maraschino cherries (optional)

1 Freeze a large bowl and a 3-quart rectangular baking dish for 15 minutes or until very cold. Meanwhile, in a medium bowl combine crushed cookies and melted butter; set aside.

2 Place ice cream in the cold bowl and press against side of bowl with a wooden spoon to soften slightly. Spoon ice cream into chilled baking dish; press ice cream into even layer in bottom of baking dish. Sprinkle cookie mixture over ice cream. Top with peanuts. Place ice cream topping in a self-sealing plastic bag; cut a small hole in one corner. Drizzle topping over layers in baking dish. Cover and freeze for at least 4 hours or until firm.

3 To serve, let stand at room temperature for 10 minutes to soften slightly. If desired, top with banana slices and maraschino cherries. Cut and serve at once.

Nutrition Facts per serving: 457 cal., 26 g total fat (12 g sat. fat), 81 mg chol., 406 mg sodium, 51 g carbo., 1 g fiber, 6 g pro.
Daily Values: 13% vit. A, 1% vit. C, 9% calcium, 6% iron

Frozen Berry Yogurt

Here's a good dessert that you can make ahead of time and serve with fresh fruit that you cut up just before dinner.

Prep: 15 minutes Chill: several hours Freeze: 30 minutes Ripen: 4 hours
Makes: 1½ quarts (6 to 8 servings)

- 1¼ cups sugar
- 1 cup water
- 3 cups fresh raspberries, blackberries, and/or strawberries
- 3 8-ounce cartons vanilla yogurt
- 1 teaspoon vanilla
- Fresh melon or other fruit, cut into thin slices (optional)

1 In a medium saucepan combine sugar and water. Cook and stir over medium-high heat until mixture comes to a boil and sugar dissolves. Remove from heat; cool.

2 In a blender combine half of the sugar mixture and berries; cover and blend until almost smooth. Pour into a fine-mesh sieve set over a bowl. Repeat with remaining sugar mixture and berries. Press berry mixture through sieve; discard seeds. Transfer berry mixture to a large bowl. Stir in yogurt and vanilla; mix until well combined. Cover and chill in the refrigerator several hours or overnight.

3 Freeze mixture in a 2-quart ice-cream freezer according to manufacturer's directions. Ripen 4 hours. If desired, cut melon or other fruit into long, thin ribbons with a vegetable peeler. Serve with scoops of frozen yogurt mixture.

Nutrition Facts per serving: 283 cal., 2 g total fat (1 g sat. fat), 6 mg chol., 76 mg sodium, 63 g carbo., 4 g fiber, 6 g pro.
Daily Values: 3% vit. A, 27% vit. C, 21% calcium, 3% iron

Mango-Raspberry Granita

Cool off the end of a piping hot, slow-cooked meal with this frozen dessert. You can let the frozen mixture soften slightly at room temperature while you're enjoying dinner.

Prep: 20 minutes Freeze: 1 hour plus several hours Stand: 5 minutes Makes: 4 servings

1 cup water
½ cup sugar
1 12-ounce package frozen lightly sweetened red raspberries
1 medium mango, peeled, seeded, and chopped
Fresh red raspberries (optional)

1 In a medium saucepan combine water and sugar. Cook and stir over medium heat until mixture just comes to a boil and sugar dissolves. Remove from heat and add the raspberries and mango. Pour into a blender or food processor. Cover and blend or process until mixture is smooth. Strain through a fine-mesh sieve (should have about 2 cups sieved fruit mixture); discard seeds.

2 Pour sieved mixture into a 13×9×2-inch baking dish or freezer container. Cover and freeze for 1 to 2 hours or until mixture is nearly frozen. Stir well, scraping frozen mixture from sides of dish or container. Spread mixture to evenly cover bottom of dish or container. Cover and freeze several hours or overnight.

3 To serve, let stand at room temperature for 5 to 10 minutes. Use an ice cream scoop to serve into dessert dishes. If desired, top with fresh raspberries.

Nutrition Facts per serving: 214 cal., 0 g total fat (0 g sat. fat), 0 mg chol., 4 mg sodium, 56 g carbo., 2 g fiber, 0 g pro.
Daily Values: 41% vit. A, 48% vit. C, 2% calcium, 3% iron

Index

Metric Information

The charts on this page provide a guide for converting measurements from the U.S. customary system, which is used throughout this book, to the metric system.

Product Differences

Most of the ingredients called for in the recipes in this book are available in most countries. However, some are known by different names. Here are some common American ingredients and their possible counterparts:

- Sugar (white) is granulated, fine granulated, or castor sugar.
- Powdered sugar is icing sugar.
- All-purpose flour is enriched, bleached or unbleached white household flour. When self-rising flour is used in place of all-purpose flour in a recipe that calls for leavening, omit the leavening agent (baking soda or baking powder) and salt.
- Light-colored corn syrup is golden syrup.
- Cornstarch is cornflour.
- Baking soda is bicarbonate of soda.
- Vanilla or vanilla extract is vanilla essence.
- Green, red, or yellow sweet peppers are capsicums or bell peppers.
- Golden raisins are sultanas.

Volume and Weight

The United States traditionally uses cup measures for liquid and solid ingredients. The chart below shows the approximate imperial and metric equivalents. If you are accustomed to weighing solid ingredients, the following approximate equivalents will be helpful.

- 1 cup butter, castor sugar, or rice = 8 ounces = ½ pound = 250 grams
- 1 cup flour = 4 ounces = ¼ pound = 125 grams
- 1 cup icing sugar = 5 ounces = 150 grams

Canadian and U.S. volume for a cup measure is 8 fluid ounces (237 ml), but the standard metric equivalent is 250 ml.

1 British imperial cup is 10 fluid ounces.

In Australia, 1 tablespoon equals 20 ml, and there are 4 teaspoons in the Australian tablespoon.

Spoon measures are used for smaller amounts of ingredients. Although the size of the tablespoon varies slightly in different countries, for practical purposes and for recipes in this book, a straight substitution is all that's necessary. Measurements made using cups or spoons always should be level unless stated otherwise.

Common Weight Range Replacements

Imperial / U.S.	Metric
½ ounce	15 g
1 ounce	25 g or 30 g
4 ounces (¼ pound)	115 g or 125 g
8 ounces (½ pound)	225 g or 250 g
16 ounces (1 pound)	450 g or 500 g
1¼ pounds	625 g
1½ pounds	750 g
2 pounds or 2¼ pounds	1,000 g or 1 Kg

Oven Temperature Equivalents

Fahrenheit Setting	Celsius Setting*	Gas Setting
300°F	150°C	Gas Mark 2 (very low)
325°F	160°C	Gas Mark 3 (low)
350°F	180°C	Gas Mark 4 (moderate)
375°F	190°C	Gas Mark 5 (moderate)
400°F	200°C	Gas Mark 6 (hot)
425°F	220°C	Gas Mark 7 (hot)
450°F	230°C	Gas Mark 8 (very hot)
475°F	240°C	Gas Mark 9 (very hot)
500°F	260°C	Gas Mark 10 (extremely hot)
Broil	Broil	Grill

*Electric and gas ovens may be calibrated using celsius. However, for an electric oven, increase celsius setting 10 to 20 degrees when cooking above 160°C. For convection or forced air ovens (gas or electric) lower the temperature setting 25°F/10°C when cooking at all heat levels.

Baking Pan Sizes

Imperial / U.S.	Metric
9×1½-inch round cake pan	22- or 23×4-cm (1.5 L)
9×1½-inch pie plate	22- or 23×4-cm (1 L)
8×8×2-inch square cake pan	20×5-cm (2 L)
9×9×2-inch square cake pan	22- or 23×4.5-cm (2.5 L)
11×7×1½-inch baking pan	28×17×4-cm (2 L)
2-quart rectangular baking pan	30×19×4.5-cm (3 L)
13×9×2-inch baking pan	34×22×4.5-cm (3.5 L)
15×10×1-inch jelly roll pan	40×25×2-cm
9×5×3-inch loaf pan	23×13×8-cm (2 L)
2-quart casserole	2 L

U.S. / Standard Metric Equivalents

⅛ teaspoon = 0.5 ml
¼ teaspoon = 1 ml
½ teaspoon = 2 ml
1 teaspoon = 5 ml
1 tablespoon = 15 ml
2 tablespoons = 25 ml
¼ cup = 2 fluid ounces = 50 ml
⅓ cup = 3 fluid ounces = 75 ml
½ cup = 4 fluid ounces = 125 ml
⅔ cup = 5 fluid ounces = 150 ml
¾ cup = 6 fluid ounces = 175 ml
1 cup = 8 fluid ounces = 250 ml
2 cups = 1 pint = 500 ml
1 quart = 1 litre